"Now I Get It!"

12 Ten-Minute Classroom Drama Skits for Science, Math, Language, and Social Studies

Volume Two for Grades 4–6

by L.E. McCullough, Ph.D.

FOCUSED LEARNING EXERCISES
TO BOOST COMPREHENSION AND CREATIVITY
IN THE ELEMENTARY CLASSROOM

YOUNG ACTORS SERIES

A Smith and Kraus Book

A Smith and Kraus Book
Published by Smith and Kraus, Inc.
177 Lyme Road, Hanover, NH 03755

First Edition: September 2000
10 9 8 7 6 5 4 3 2 1

Cover and Text Design by Julia Hill Gignoux, Freedom Hill Design
Cover Photo: Students at the Theatre School of Indianapolis prepare a
presentation with intructor Richard Merriman.
Photo by L.E. McCullough.

The Library of Congress Cataloging-In-Publication Data
McCullough, L.E.
Now I get it! : 12 ten-minute classroom drama skits for science, math,
language, and social studies / by L.E. McCullough. —1st ed.
p. cm. — (Young actors series)
"Focused learning exercises to boost comprehension and creativity
in the elementary classroom."
Contents: v.1. For grades K–3 — v.2. For grades 4–6.
ISBN 1-57525-161-2 (vol.1) — ISBN 1-57525-162-0 (vol.2)
1. Children's plays, American. 2. Drama in education.
I. Title. II. Young actor series.
PS3563.C35297 N69 2000
812'.54—dc21   00-058778

This book is dedicated to all my teachers throughout my life, beginning with my parents, Ervin and Isabel McCullough. Looking back, I wish I knew then what I know now but didn't have a clue I'd ever need to know. (Guess that's what teachers are for. . .)

CONTENTS

Foreword

Education is a social process. Education is growth.
Education is not preparation for life. Education is life itself.
John Dewey, Educator

Good teaching is one-fourth preparation and three-
fourths theatre.
Gail Godwin, Author

The greatest sign of success for a teacher is to be able to
say, "The children are now working as if I did not exist."
Maria Montessori, Educator

One of the most profound concepts to have emerged in educational philosophy during the last decade is the realization that people have different, equally valid ways of learning. Based on their own unique experiences, frames of reference, prior knowledge and cognitive skills and structures, different individuals possess different "intelligences" and will understand and utilize information differently.

Some people learn more easily by visual reference, others by focusing on auditory cues. Some learn best by reading and rote memorization, others by hands-on doing and problem-solving tasks. It has become clear that, along the daily journey of acquiring knowledge, there are many paths to the same goal.

The challenge for today's educator — at any grade level — is to create an interactive and collaborative learning environment that can accommodate students' varying "intelligences." Drama, with its inherent capacity to tap and synthesize a wide range of skills and expressive modes, is a highly effective way of achieving this goal.

The plays in the "*Now* I Get It!" series are short drama pieces designed to help teachers convey basic curriculum material in Science, Math, Language and Social Studies. While almost any play can be used in some way to complement or illustrate a particular topic at hand, the "*Now* I Get It!" plays are specifically designed to serve as focused learning exercises to boost comprehension and creativity in the elementary classroom.

I've called these plays *skits,* not to downgrade their utility or seriousness of purpose but rather to reassure teachers that one need not be a trained drama specialist to make effective use of basic theatrical techniques in the classroom. There are several dictionary definitions of *skit*; the one I prefer is "a short dramatic piece, especially one done by amateurs,"[1] possibly derived from an 18th-century English dialect term *skite*, meaning "to move quickly" — which is exactly what a well-written, well-executed skit does.

As an aid to curriculum development during the last decade, many state education departments have adopted basic standards or "proficiencies" in each subject area. These proficiencies are goals for student learning that emphasize specific concepts and skills; teachers are free to organize methods of instruction to best meet their students' needs.

In the State of Indiana, where I currently reside, the Indiana Department of Education has cited the following eight proficiencies in English/Language Arts[2] :

- exhibiting a positive attitude toward language and learning
- selecting and applying effective strategies for reading
- comprehending developmentally appropriate materials
- select and using developmentally appropriate strategies for writing

- writing for different purposes and audiences producing a variety of forms
- using prior knowledge and content area information to make critical judgments
- communicating orally with people of all ages
- recognizing the interrelatedness of language, literature and culture

In effect, each English/Language Arts course at every grade level should contribute to aiding students in attaining these proficiencies. Drama facilitates this process by being an *elastic* and *inclusive* medium that offers students a firm organizational structure along with the freedom to reshape that structure into a wholly new learning experience.

Each *"Now* I Get It!*"* play is accompanied by a list of suggested pre- and post-play activities and discussion questions; consider these plays foundations and stepping stones for further research and learning by your students. Though each play script is self-contained and based on actual lesson material, the format allows for additional information you might want to insert. Obviously, a short skit can cover nothing more than the basic outline of a lesson and the merest surface of a topic. I have supplied only rudimentary stage and lighting directions. Use your imagination to expand or adapt the plays for your classroom space, your student population, your curriculum needs. Then, once you've got the hang of it, have students write their own plays for other lessons!

If you're a teacher, the *"Now* I Get It!*"* plays are a great way of imparting basic knowledge to students, then inspiring them to discover more on their own. For parents, at-home production of the plays helps parents and children achieve a "good goal" together. Parents get to see their children at their most vibrant and creative. Children get to excel for their parents, and they become more self-motivated and self-reliant, especially in terms of socializing with other children. By going through the process of creating and interpreting a play for an audience — even if the audience is only the family or the classroom — adults and children learn to listen to each other better.

And for kids, is there really any better way to learn the rules of grammar than by playing a dancing participle?

L.E. McCullough, Ph.D.
Humanities Theatre Group
Indiana University-Purdue University at Indianapolis
Indianapolis, Indiana

---

[1] *Merriam Webster's Collegiate Dictionary*, 10th Edition, 1993.
[2] *English/Language Arts Proficiency Guide: Essential Skills for Indiana Students*, Indiana Department of Education, 1999.

Acknowledgments

Terry Porter, Agape Productions; Julie Pratt McQuiston, *Arts Indiana*; Anne Laker, POLIS Center at Indiana University-Purdue University at Indianapolis; Administrative Service Center, Washington Township Schools, Indianapolis; Curriculum and Instruction Division, Indianapolis Public Schools; Jane Hughes Gignoux; J.J. Stenzoski and Rush Yelverton of the Downtown Kiwanis Club; Alan Cloe, WFYI-TV; Maureen Dobie of NUVO Newsweekly; Susan Cross, Woodward High School, Cincinnati; Debra, Ryan, and Michael Kelleher; Miss Jeanne Grubb, my father's first piano teacher, now 96 years young.

language arts

THE ALMIGHTY APOSTROPHE
(Syntax)

Basic Concept:

This play introduces the *apostrophe* and its usage with *verb and pronoun contractions*.

Pre- or Post-Play Activities:

• Have students make a list with two columns: Column A lists all the pronoun contractions they can think of and Column B lists the two words that comprise the contraction. Then have students practice going back and forth between the contracted and un-contracted versions. Are there any exceptions to the basic rules for apostrophe use with pronouns?

• Now do the same with verb contractions: Column A lists all the verb contractions students can think of and Column B lists the two words that comprise the contraction. Then have students practice going back and forth between the contracted and un-contracted versions. Are there any exceptions to the basic rules for apostrophe use with verbs?

Discussion Questions:

• Do other languages besides English use the apostrophe? How do they use it? Do they use it for verb and pronoun contractions?

• The use of the apostrophe as a contraction came into the English language during the 18th century. Why do you think this occurred? What would our everyday speech be like if there were no verb and pronoun contractions?

2

STAGE SET: at mid center an old-time general store with a counter, some shelves stocked with books; a banner stretched overhead reading "The Grammar Store — Words 'R' Us" and some signs taped on the counter front or shelves or scrim reading "Irregular Verbs, 30% Off," "New-Model Commas Just Arrived!," "Fresh Antonyms for Home and Garden"

CAST: 8 actors, min. 1 boy (•), 1 girl (+)

+ Miss Construe, Store Clerk
• Hank, A Customer
Store Clerks 1-6

PROPS: several cardboard signs; application form; pen

MUSIC: *The Apostrophe Song; Hi, There, Hank!*

COSTUMES: Hank wears contemporary school clothes; Miss Construe wears an old-time general store clerk's outfit — dress shirt, suspenders, bow tie, name tag on shirt, perhaps an eye-visor hat; Customers can wear contemporary school clothes — or — have each Customer attired in a strange costume. . .a football player, a farmer, an airplane pilot, a ballerina, a cowboy, an astronaut. . .use your imagination!

Hi, There, Hank!
(traditional, arranged by L.E. McCullough)

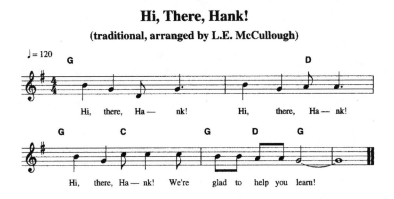

The Apostrophe Song

(words & music by L.E. McCullough)

An a- pos- tro- phe is a beau- ti- ful
thing, a han- dy, dan- dy, most du- ti- ful
thing. It is ea- sy to use when- ev- er you
choose to leave out a let- ter and bring words to-
ge- ther. An a- pos- tro- phe is a
glor- i- ous thing, a root- in', toot- in' no-

The Apostrophe Song, pg. 2

tor- i- ous thing. It tells you what's what and to

whom it be- longs, the al- migh- ty a- pos- tro- phe —

sim- ple and strong!

* when sung at end of play, use
  ending below starting at this measure

pos- tro- phe, you'll al- ways be boss to me, an a-

pos- tro- phe ne- ver goes wrong!

© L.E. McCullough 2000

(LIGHTS UP FULL ON MISS CONSTRUE behind counter, stacking books on shelves, whistling idly. HANK, a customer, enters from left and tentatively crosses to center.)

MISS CONSTRUE: *(loudly, aggressively)* Good morning, sir! Welcome to The Grammar Store! I'm Miss Construe, owner and CEO.

HANK: *(a bit startled)* CEO?

MISS CONSTRUE: That stands for Chief Educational Officer. How may I be of service?

HANK: Umm, I'd like a, uh, umm. . .

MISS CONSTRUE: I'm sorry, sir, speak up please! Can't hear you!

HANK: Umm—

MISS CONSTRUE: Here at The Grammar Store we have the finest selection of low-price, high-quality grammar tools for home and office. Thirty per cent off on irregular verbs — just till Tuesday! Would you like to try on a brand new pair of parentheses? I'm sure we have one in your size!

HANK: I, ummm, I'd like to buy an apostrophe.

MISS CONSTRUE: *(turns serious)* An apostrophe.

HANK: Is there an echo in here?

MISS CONSTRUE: We don't carry echoes, sir. Check the Sound Wave Shoppe on the corner.

HANK: I don't want an echo, I want an apostrophe.

MISS CONSTRUE: So you said. For your information, sir, we don't sell our apostrophes to just anybody off the street.

HANK: I beg your—

MISS CONSTRUE: How do we know you'll use your apostrophe in a responsible fashion?

HANK: Well, I—

MISS CONSTRUE: How do we know you'll keep your apostrophe clean and well-fed?

HANK: Well, I—

MISS CONSTRUE: How do we know you can even *handle* a real apostrophe?

HANK: Well, I—

(Miss Construe pulls a piece of paper and pen from behind counter and sets them on the countertop.)

MISS CONSTRUE: You'll need to get an Apostrophe Approval License.

HANK: What?

MISS CONSTRUE: Here is your Application to Apply for an Application for an Apostrophe Approval License.

HANK: This is crazy! All I want is an ordinary apostrophe!

MISS CONSTRUE: Sir, there *is* no such thing as an "ordinary apostrophe." Name?

HANK: None of your beeswax!

MISS CONSTRUE: Can you spell that, please?

HANK: No, that's not my name, look—

MISS CONSTRUE: Name?

HANK: Sorry. Hank.

MISS CONSTRUE: Hank? That's your name? Hank?

HANK: Is there an — never mind. Yes, my name *is* Hank!

MISS CONSTRUE: And my name is Pocahontas. All right, Mr. *Hank*, just why do you want an apostrophe?

HANK: I, umm, I, uh, I've heard an apostrophe will make me look really cool.

MISS CONSTRUE: Hank, Hank, Hank. . .you don't use an apostrophe to enhance your appearance.

HANK: You don't?

MISS CONSTRUE: No, Hank. You use an apostrophe to mark a contraction or a possessive — and to pluralize letters and numerals.

HANK: Really? I see.

MISS CONSTRUE: Indeed! *(shouts toward offstage right)* Customer Service to the front!

(STORE CLERKS 1-6 enter from right carrying several cardboard signs and singing. MUSIC: "The Apostrophe Song.")

STORE CLERKS 1-3: *(singing)* An apostrophe is a beautiful thing,

STORE CLERKS 4-6: *(singing)* A handy, dandy, most dutiful thing.

STORE CLERKS 1-3: *(singing)* It is easy to use whenever you choose

STORE CLERKS 4-6: *(singing)* To leave out a letter and bring words together.

STORE CLERKS 1-2: *(singing)* An apostrophe is a glorious thing,

STORE CLERKS 3-4: *(singing)* A rootin', tootin', notorious thing.

STORE CLERKS 5-6: *(singing)* It tells you what's what and to whom it belongs,

STORE CLERKS 1-6: *(singing)* The almighty apostrophe — simple and strong!

(Store Clerks 1-3 stand to right of counter; Store Clerks 4-6 stand to left of counter.)

MISS CONSTRUE: Associates, this is Hank.

(STORE CLERKS 1-6 sing. MUSIC: "Hi, There, Hank.")

STORE CLERKS 1-6: *(singing)* Hi there, Hank. Hi, there, Hank. Hi, there, Hank, we're glad to help you learn!

MISS CONSTRUE: First of all, Hank, do you know how to spell "apostrophe"?

HANK: I think so. *(slowly)* A-P-O-S-T-R-O-P-H-E.

MISS CONSTRUE: Again, please.

HANK: Apostrophe. A-P-O-S-T-R-O-P-H-E. Apostrophe.

STORE CLERKS 1-6: *(applauding)* Go, Hank! Go, Hank! Goooooooooo, Hank!

MISS CONSTRUE: Excellent! The first use of the apostrophe we'll look at is when the apostrophe makes a contraction with a verb and the word "not."

STORE CLERK 1: A contraction is a shortened form of two words.

STORE CLERK 2: Two words are made into one word.

STORE CLERK 3: With an apostrophe taking the place of the letter or letters left out to form the new word.

(Store Clerk 1 shows sign reading "is.")

STORE CLERK 1: Is.

(Store Clerk 2 shows sign reading "not.")

STORE CLERK 2: Not.

(Store Clerk 3 shows sign reading "isn't.")

STORE CLERK 3: And now the contraction — "isn't." Spelled I-S-N-apostrophe-T.

HANK: *(points to apostrophe on Store Clerk 3's sign)* And there is the apostrophe! It replaced the letter "o" in "not."

MISS CONSTRUE: Very good, Hank. You're a quick learner. Show him some more verb contractions!

(Store Clerk 1 shows sign reading "was.")

STORE CLERK 1: Was.

(Store Clerk 2 shows sign reading "not.")

STORE CLERK 2: Not.

(Store Clerk 3 shows sign reading "wasn't.")

STORE CLERK 3: And now the contraction — "wasn't." Spelled W-A-S-N-apostrophe-T.

HANK: *(points to apostrophe on Store Clerk 3's sign)* The apostrophe replaced the letter "o" in "not."

MISS CONSTRUE: Which it will do every time!

(Store Clerk 1 shows sign reading "could.")

STORE CLERK 1: Could.

(Store Clerk 2 shows sign reading "not.")

STORE CLERK 2: Not.

(Store Clerk 3 shows sign reading "couldn't.")

STORE CLERK 3: And now the contraction — "couldn't."

HANK: Spelled C-O-U-L-D-N-apostrophe-T. The apostrophe replaced the letter "o" in "not."

MISS CONSTRUE: Good job, Hank! And don't forget: the apostrophe in a verb contraction always goes between the "n" and the "t."

HANK: Always?

STORE CLERKS 1-6: Always!

HANK: *(picks up application form from counter)* Great! If that's all there is to the apostrophe, maybe I could pick up—

MISS CONSTRUE: *(snatches form from Hank's hand)* Not so fast! All there is to the apostrophe?

STORE CLERKS 1-6: Hah!

MISS CONSTRUE: We've barely begun!

STORE CLERKS 1-6: Hah!

MISS CONSTRUE: There's the little matter of *pronoun contractions.*

STORE CLERK 4: A pronoun contraction joins a pronoun and a verb.

STORE CLERK 5: Once again, two words are made into one word.

STORE CLERK 6: With an apostrophe taking the place of the letter or letters left out to form the new word.

(Store Clerk 4 shows sign reading "I.")

STORE CLERK 4: I — a pronoun.

(Store Clerk 5 shows sign reading "am.")

STORE CLERK 5: Am — a verb.

(Store Clerk 6 shows sign reading "I'm.")

STORE CLERK 6: And now the contraction — "I'm." Spelled I-apostrophe-M.

HANK: *(points to apostrophe on Store Clerk 6's sign)* And there is the apostrophe! It replaced the letter "a" in "am."

MISS CONSTRUE: Will wonders never cease?

(Store Clerk 4 shows sign reading "we.")

STORE CLERK 4: We — a pronoun.

(Store Clerk 5 shows sign reading "are.")

STORE CLERK 5: Are — a verb.

(Store Clerk 6 shows sign reading "we're.")

STORE CLERK 6: And now the contraction — "we're." Spelled W-E-apostrophe-R-E.

HANK: *(points to apostrophe on Store Clerk 6's sign)* And there is the apostrophe! It replaced the letter "a" in "are."

MISS CONSTRUE: He's on a roll!

(Store Clerk 4 shows sign reading "you.")

STORE CLERK 4: You — a pronoun.

(Store Clerk 5 shows sign reading "have.")

STORE CLERK 5: Have — a verb.

(Store Clerk 6 shows sign reading "you've.")

STORE CLERK 6: And now the contraction — "you've." Spelled Y-O-U-apostrophe-V-E.

HANK: *(points to apostrophe on Store Clerk 6's sign)* And there is the apostrophe! It replaced two letters — the letter "h" and the letter "a" in "have." Can the apostrophe do that?

MISS CONSTRUE: Try and stop it!

(Store Clerk 6 shows sign reading "she'd.")

STORE CLERK 6: Here's a pronoun contraction — "she'd."

HANK: S-H-E-apostrophe-D.

STORE CLERK 6: How many letters did this apostrophe replace?

HANK: Wow, that's a brain-buster!

MISS CONSTRUE: Give the cusotmer some assistance, please!

(Store Clerk 4 shows sign reading "she.")

STORE CLERK 4: She — a pronoun.
(Store Clerk 5 shows sign reading "would.")

STORE CLERK 5: Would — a verb.

STORE CLERK 6: Make the contraction, and the two words "she" and "would" become—

HANK: "She'd"! S-H-E-apostrophe-D. That apostrophe took out the "w," the "o," the "u" and the "l" in "would." One, two, three, four letters gone!

STORE CLERK 1: Astonishing!

STORE CLERK 2: Amazing!

STORE CLERK 3: Appealing!

STORE CLERK 4: Arresting!

STORE CLERK 5: Amusing!

STORE CLERK 6: Absorbing!

MISS CONSTRUE: The almighty apostrophe strikes again!

(Store Clerks 1–6 and Hank applaud and cheer.)

HANK: *(points to application form held by Miss Construe)* Now, about me buying an apostrophe. . .

MISS CONSTRUE: *(withholds form)* Ohhhhh, no, Mr. Hurry-Up-And-Gimme-An-Apostrophe-Before-I-Jump-Out-Of-My-Skin Hank! We've only covered the use of the apostrophe in contractions.

HANK: There's more!?!

MISS CONSTRUE: Prepare yourself forrrrrrr — possessives!

HANK: This could take all day!

MISS CONSTRUE: An apostrophe in the wrong hands is a very, very bad thing. But you're right, Hank — we've had a good grammar workout! Let's take a rest and start on possessives tomorrow!

HANK: Tomorrow!?! I told my friends I'd have a brand new apostrophe for the party tonight!

STORE CLERKS 1-6: Tonight!

HANK: Well, can we at least sing *The Apostrophe Song* one more time?

MISS CONSTRUE: That request we can meet! *(to audience)*
And you all can sing with us! Take it away, maestro!

(Everyone sings. MUSIC: "The Apostrophe Song.")

ALL: *(singing)* An apostrophe is a beautiful thing,
A handy, dandy, most dutiful thing.
It is easy to use whenever you choose
To leave out a letter and bring words together.

An apostrophe is a glorious thing,
A rootin', tootin', notorious thing.
It tells you what's what and to whom it belongs,
The almighty apostrophe,
You'll always be boss to me
An apostrophe never goes wrong!

(LIGHTS OUT)

THE END

LET'S WRITE A POEM!
(Writing)

Basic Concept:

This play introduces the basic elements of *poetry* and related terms such as *meter, rhyme, limerick, haiku* and *free verse*.

Pre- or Post-Play Activities:

- Have students make a list of things that interest them; then choose one topic and write a poem about it.

- Make a list of phrases from proverbs, songs or everyday speech ("early bird gets the worm," "somewhere over the rainbow," "give us our daily bread," "later, alligator," etc.) and have students write poems using them as a subject or phrase.

- Have students view pictures from a news magazine without the caption, then write a poem about the picture.

Discussion Questions:

- Have students read their favorite poem; ask them to describe what it is about the poem they like.

- Read a short poem and ask students to change just one word; have them explain why they changed this word, then talk about how this one-word change alters the meaning of the poem.

STAGE SET: A classroom — at mid center is a chalkboard with 5 chairs grouped on the left, 5 chairs on the right, the chairs facing audience at a 45° angle

CAST: 11 actors, min. 6 boys (•), 5 girls (+)

+ Rosanna	• Christopher
+ Joan	• Stephen
+ Melody	• Gary
+ Karen	• Marcus
+ Andrea	• Oliver
	• Mr. Moreland, Teacher

PROPS: chalk; chalk eraser

COSTUMES: characters wear contemporary school clothes

(LIGHTS UP FULL ON MR. MORELAND, the teacher, at mid center in front of the chalkboard addressing a class.)

MR. MORELAND: And that is how you correct a run-on sentence. Who can make the first example into a correct sentence?

(A student, ROSANNA, scribbles a note and passes it to her neighbor, CHRISTOPHER, who reads it and snickers loudly.)

MR. MORELAND: Christopher?

CHRISTOPHER: *(snaps to attention)* Fourteen divided by three is twelve!

(Class giggles.)

MR. MORELAND: Not only is that the wrong answer, Christopher, it's the wrong question — and the wrong subject! What do you have in your hand?

CHRISTOPHER: Uhhhhhh, it's a piece of paper, Mr. Moreland.

MR. MORELAND: And where did you get the piece of paper, Christopher?

CHRISTOPHER: Uhhhhhh—

ROSANNA: *(raises her hand)* He got it from me, sir.

MR. MORELAND: In this classroom, Rosanna, only teachers hand out papers. What does the paper say, Christopher?

CHRISTOPHER: Uhhhhhh—

ROSANNA: It's a poem, sir. I was practicing my writing skills.

MR. MORELAND: A poem, excellent! Please read Rosanna's poem to the class, Christopher.

CHRISTOPHER: Uhhhhhh—

ROSANNA: *(sighs)* It says, "Roses are red, violets are blue; your face is funny, and you smell funny, too!"

(Class roars with laughter; Mr. Moreland maintains a serious expression.)

ROSANNA: *(stands)* I'm sorry for disrupting the class, Mr. Moreland. I'll go to the principal's office now.
MR. MORELAND: Hold on, Rosanna. Sit down, please. Since you've brought up the subject, let's talk about poetry. What is a poem? Who knows?

(JOAN raises her hand.)

MR. MORELAND: Joan.
JOAN: A poem is a thought or an idea.
MR. MORELAND: A poem is a thought or an idea. That's true, but a sentence and a paragraph can also express a thought or idea. What makes a poem different?

(STEPHEN raises his hand.)

MR. MORELAND: Stephen.
STEPHEN: A poem is made up of lines.
MR. MORELAND: That's right. And when those lines are all together, we call them "verse." *(writes "verse" on board)* A poem is a thought or an idea expressed in verse.
STEPHEN: Each line of a poem has to end with a word that rhymes with another line.
MR. MORELAND: There are many kinds of rhyme patterns. And some poems don't rhyme at all. But what does the word "rhyme" mean?

(MELODY raises her hand; Mr. Moreland writes "rhyme" on board.)

MR. MORELAND: Melody.

MELODY: A rhyme is when two words sound the same at the end.

MR. MORELAND: Can you give an example?

MELODY: Like "bear" and "care." Or "flow" and "go."

MR. MORELAND: That's right. And a rhyme can have more than one syllable be the same, can't it?

(GARY raises his hand.)

MR. MORELAND: Gary.

GARY: "Fishing" and "wishing."

MR. MORELAND: That's two syllables. Who knows a rhyme with three syllables?

(KAREN raises her hand.)

MR. MORELAND: Karen.

KAREN: "Wandering" and "pondering."

MR. MORELAND: Excellent. All right, class. Listen to this poem:

Humpty Dumpty sat on a wall.
Humpty Dumpty had a great fall.
All the king's horses and all the king's men
Couldn't put Humpty Dumpty together again.

What do you notice about this poem?

(MARCUS raises his hand.)

MR. MORELAND: Marcus.

MARCUS: The first and second lines rhyme with each other.

MR. MORELAND: "Wall" and "fall."

MARCUS: And then the third and fourth lines rhyme.

MR. MORELAND: "Men" and "again." Good. Here's a poem by the early 20th-century American poet Langston

Hughes. It's called *Trip: San Francisco*. Listen and decide what is unique about this rhyme pattern.

I went to San Francisco.
I saw the bridges high,
Spun across the water
Like cobwebs in the sky.

(ANDREA raises her hand.)

MR. MORELAND: Yes, Andrea.
ANDREA: In this poem, the second line rhymes with the fourth.
MR. MORELAND: "High" and "sky."
ANDREA: But the first and third lines don't rhyme at all.
MR. MORELAND: That's all right. The more poems you read, the more you discover that there are many types of rhyme patterns. Here's a type of poem I'm sure you've heard before:

There was an old man of Kilkenny
Who never had more than a penny;
He spent all his money
On onions and honey;
That silly old man of Kilkenny.

(Class laughs; OLIVER raises his hand.)

MR. MORELAND: Oliver.
OLIVER: That type of poem is called a "limerick."
MR. MORELAND: *(writes "limerick" on board)* Yes, it is. Limerick is a city in southwest Ireland, and during the 1700s this type of poem became associated with that town. In the 1800s an English poet named Edward Lear wrote hundreds of limericks and made it even more popular. What was the rhyme pattern here?

(Rosanna raises her hand.)

MR. MORELAND: Rosanna.

ROSANNA: It had five lines. Lines one and two and five rhymed with each other. And lines three and four rhymed.

MR. MORELAND: Very good. That is the basic rhyme pattern of a limerick. What else did you notice about this poem?

(Karen raises her hand.)

MR. MORELAND: Karen.

KAREN: The way you said the words. There was a rhythm like "da-DA-da-da-DA-da-da-DA-da" — "there *was* an old *man* of Kil*ken*ny."

MR. MORELAND: That's right. Anyone else notice that rhythm? We all know that music has rhythm. So does poetry. And rhythm in poetry consists of the syllables sounding in a regular pattern, a pattern made by repetition. Can anyone think of lines they've heard from a poem that have rhythm?

(Gary raises his hand.)

MR. MORELAND: Gary.

GARY: Two, four, six, eight; who do we appreciate?

MR. MORELAND: That's good. If we were singing that as a piece of music, it would be in four-four time and be counted like this, Say it again, Gary, and I'll count time with you.

(Gary recites the lines as Mr. Moreland taps a four-four beat on the chalkboard.)

GARY:	MR. MORELAND:
Two, four, six, eight;	One, two, three, four;
Who do we appreciate?	One, two, three, four.

MR. MORELAND: Those two lines of poetry count off the same as two measures of music. Which is why that little poem is so popular as a cheer because it is so strongly rhythmic. *(writes "meter" on board)* The rhythmic pattern of a poem is called its *meter*. Here is another type of syllable pattern:

> In the fall birds sing;
> Brown leaves fall from bright tall trees.
> I love fall, don't you?

That's pretty, isn't it? I'll say this poem again, and this time, count the syllables in each line.

> In the fall birds sing;
> Brown leaves fall from bright tall trees.
> I love fall, don't you?

(Joan raises her hand.)

MR. MORELAND: Joan.

JOAN: The first line had five syllables. The second line had seven syllables. And the third line had five syllables.

MR. MORELAND: That's right. *(writes "haiku" on board)* This is a type of poem from Japan called "haiku," and it has a syllable pattern just as Joan described. First line, five syllables; second line, seven syllables; third line; five syllables. A haiku is sort of a quick thought or fleeting impression, something a poet sees or feels at a particular moment. Can anyone think of a haiku?

(Andrea raises her hand.)

MR. MORELAND: Andrea.

ANDREA: My cat says "meow"
Every time I feed him—
Cat talk for "thank you."

(Class laughs.)

MR. MORELAND: That's very good, Andrea. Very clever. And do the syllables count out right? Say it again, Andrea, and we'll count with you.

ANDREA: My cat says "meow"
Every time I feed him—
Cat talk for "thank you."

MR. MORELAND: Five syllables in line one, seven syllables in line two and five syllables again in line three. Congratulations, Andrea, you've just composed a haiku! Let's have some applause for Andrea!

(Class applauds.)

MR. MORELAND: Sometimes a poem doesn't rhyme or have a repeated line pattern or a specific pattern of syllables or even a strong rhythm. This kind of a poem is called free verse. *(writes "free verse" on board)* But remember what we said to start with — what is a poem?

(Stephen raises his hand.)

MR. MORELAND: Stephen.

STEPHEN: A poem is a thought or an idea expressed in verse.

MR. MORELAND: A poem is a thought or an idea expressed in verse. And what about those thoughts and ideas? They paint pictures, don't they? They convey feelings. They look at something ordinary and describe it in an unusual way. A poem tells the writer's feelings about a particular subject at a particular moment in time the way no one else but the writer can see it, hear it, feel, taste or smell it. A poem is like a small machine, a machine made of words that has a specific purpose — to express a thought or idea. So, how do we build a poem? What's the first thing we have to do?

(Oliver raises his hand.)

MR. MORELAND: Oliver.

OLIVER: You have to figure out what to write about.

MR. MORELAND: That's exactly what you do. You choose a *subject* for the poem. *(writes "Building a Poem" on board with "subject" underneath)* If we take Andrea's haiku as an example, what is the subject of that poem?

(Marcus raises his hand.)

MR. MORELAND: Marcus.

MARCUS: Her cat is the subject.

MR. MORELAND: Right. Next, you open the poem with a *statement* about the subject. A question, an image, a comparison, whatever you like that says something about the subject. *(writes "statement" underneath "subject")* How did Andrea's haiku start?

(Melody raises her hand.)

MR. MORELAND: Melody.

MELODY: It started: "My cat says 'meow' every time I feed him."

MR. MORELAND: Is that a statement?

MELODY: Yes.

MR. MORELAND: "My cat says 'meow' every time I feed him" is definitely a statement, an observation, an image.

A poem also needs *details. (writes "details" underneath "statement")* Think of that other haiku:

In the fall birds sing;
Brown leaves fall from bright tall trees.
I love fall, don't you?

What kind of leaves fell?

(Christopher raises his hand.)

MR. MORELAND: Christopher.
CHRISTOPHER: Brown leaves.
MR. MORELAND: What kind of trees?
CHRISTOPHER: Bright tall trees.
MR. MORELAND: Those are very concise details that help you see the leaves and trees the way the writer sees them. Poems also provide details by making *comparisons* between one thing and another. *(writes "comparison" underneath "details")* Think about the Langston Hughes poem we heard:

I went to San Francisco.
I saw the bridges high,
Spun across the water
Like cobwebs in the sky.

Is there a comparison in this poem?

(Stephen raises his hand.)

MR. MORELAND: Stephen.
STEPHEN: The bridges are compared to cobwebs.
MR. MORELAND: Right. And that image of a spider's web gives you a new way of looking at bridges, doesn't it? Usually when you look at a bridge, it seems very big and sturdy. But seen against the whole sky stretching for miles and miles into the distance, that big powerful

bridge suddenly seems as fragile as a cobweb. The poet has made us stop a moment in our busy day and think about something ordinary from a new point of view. Can you think of anything else a poem should have?

(Joan raises her hand.)

MR. MORELAND: Joan.

JOAN: It should have a point at the end. You know, some reason the writer wrote the poem.

MR. MORELAND: Something the poet wants you to understand? A message or theme you're supposed to take with you after reading the poem?

JOAN: Yes.

MR. MORELAND: Humpty Dumpty sat on a wall.
Humpty Dumpty had a great fall.
All the king's horses and all the king's men
Couldn't put Humpty Dumpty together again.

What's the point of that poem?

(Karen raises her hand.)

MR. MORELAND: Karen.

KAREN: That Humpty Dumpty was totally broken and could never be mended.

MR. MORELAND: That's a good one. Let's call this the *conclusion*. *(writes "conclusion" underneath "comparison")* In Andrea's haiku, what was the conclusion?

(Melody raises her hand.)

MR. MORELAND: Melody.

MELODY: That "meow" was cat talk for "thank you."

MR. MORELAND: That's right. What's the conclusion in this poem:

In the fall birds sing;
Brown leaves fall from bright tall trees.
I love fall, don't you?

(Marcus raises his hand.)

MR. MORELAND: Marcus.
MARCUS: That the writer loves fall.
MR. MORELAND: Yes, and the conclusion of the limerick?

(Gary raises his hand.)

MR. MORELAND: Gary.
GARY: That the old man from Kilkenny was silly for the
   way he spent his money.
MR. MORELAND: Absolutely! Now, we need one more
   thing to finish building our poem. Can anyone guess
   what it is? Let's review. Our poem has, Joan—
JOAN: A subject.
MR. MORELAND: Andrea—
ANDREA: Opening statement.
MR. MORELAND: Oliver—
OLIVER: Details.
MR. MORELAND: Karen—
KAREN: Comparisons.
MR. MORELAND: Christopher—
CHRISTOPHER: A conclusion.
MR. MORELAND: What's missing?

(Stephen raises his hand.)

MR. MORELAND: Stephen?
STEPHEN: A title?
MR. MORELAND: A title! *(writes "title" below "conclu-
   sion" and draws arrow from "title" to above "subject")*
   The title not only helps the reader get a better sense of

what the poem is about, it also helps the writer focus on what he or she really wants to say in the poem. Sometimes it's good to start with a title before you've written the poem, just to get your thoughts centered. You can always change the title after you've finished the poem. *(looks at his watch)* Gosh, class is almost over. We've come a long way from run-on sentences, haven't we — thanks to our budding poets, Rosanna and Christopher.

(Class chuckles.)

MR. MORELAND: It just proves that learning happens in unexpected ways, and we must always be ready to learn from our experience. And for our next assignment, let's write a poem, shall we?

(Christopher raises his hand.)

MR. MORELAND: Yes, Christopher.
CHRISTOPHER: Can we write a poem about any subject?
MR. MORELAND: Yes, any subject. But with one limitation — no poem can start out with the phrase "Roses are red, violets are blue"!

(Class laughs; LIGHTS OUT.)

THE END

HOLY, HOLEY, WHOLLY COW!
HOMONYMS & HOMOPHONES
ON THE LOOSE!
(Vocabulary)

Basic Concept:

This play introduces *homonyms* and *homophones*, first defining them and then providing examples in usage.

Pre- or Post-Play Activities:

• Have students make a list of homonyms and homophones; then cut out pictures from newspapers, magazines or catalogues that show their meaning and make flash cards for pop quizzes.

• Have students make sentences using homonyms and homophones, then put the sentences together to make a story.

Discussion Questions:

• Look up several homophones in the dictionary; what are their root words? How do you think they came to be pronounced the same in English, even though they are spelled differently and have different meanings?

• Look up several homonyms in the dictionary; what are their root words? How do you think they came to be pronounced and spelled the same, even though their meanings are different? Or do you think the different meanings of the word came about before the spelling?

STAGE SET: a classroom; at mid-center are a medium-size table, a chair, a large chalkboard

CAST: students 1–8

PROPS: yard light pole; 2 pieces of chalk; 2 chalkboard erasers

COSTUMES: characters wear contemporary school clothes

*(LIGHTS UP FULL ON STUDENT 1 sitting and STU-
DENTS 2 and 3 standing at a table, writing and shuf-
fling papers; STUDENT 4 enters from left dragging a
long street sign pole.)*

STUDENT 1: What are you doing?

STUDENT 4: What am I doing? I'm playing tiddlywinks!
What does it look like I'm doing?

STUDENT 1: I asked you to bring me a poll!

STUDENT 4: And what's this in my hands? A rhinoceros?
It's a bug-zapper light pole! I found it lying by the side of
the road and dragged it all the way here! Whew, am I
tired!

STUDENT 2: But we wanted a *poll* — spelled P-O-L-L. A
poll — P-O-L-L — is a survey that asks questions about
a certain subject.

STUDENT 4: And your point is?

STUDENT 3: You've brought us a pole — spelled P-O-L-E.

STUDENT 4: Oh. Well, you can still ask questions about it.

STUDENT 1: I take it you missed the class where we learned
about *homophones* and *homonyms?*

STUDENT 4: I know all about homonyms! They were the
primate ancestors of early humans.

STUDENT 2: No! Those were *hominids* — H-O-M-I-N-I-D-S!

STUDENT 4: And your—

STUDENT 3: The point is, it's *not* the same thing.
Homonyms are two or more words spelled alike and
pronounced alike — but have different meanings.

STUDENT 1: Such as quail — Q-U-A-I-L — the bird.

STUDENT 2: And quail— Q-U-A-I-L — meaning to show
fear.

STUDENT 4: And homophones?

STUDENT 3: Homophones are two or more words pronounced alike but spelled differently. They also have different meanings.

STUDENT 1: Sometimes *very* different meanings!

Holy, Holey, Wholly Cow! 31

STUDENT 4: Such as?

STUDENT 2: Such as poll spelled P-O-L-L.

STUDENT 3: And pole spelled P-O-L-E.

(Student 4 throws hands in the air and paces as if in rapture.)

STUDENT 4: Ah, yes, I see, I see! It is all becoming very, very clear!

STUDENT 1: Do you think it's very clear?

STUDENT 2: No way!

STUDENT 3: Not at all! We need to do a grammar intervention!

STUDENT 1: Set this poor student straight!

STUDENT 2: No one can grow up without understanding homonyms and homophones!

STUDENT 3: And hope to live a *normal* life!

STUDENT 1: We may need reinforcements!

STUDENT 2: I'll get some! *(whistles loudly toward stage right)*

STUDENT 4: I understand perfectly! Homophones are special telephones attached to the hominids, when they call up room service to order dinosaur burgers!

(STUDENTS 5, 6, 7 and 8 enter from right and gather at center.)

STUDENT 3: Everybody ready!

STUDENTS 1, 2, 5, 6, 7, 8: Ready!

(Their loud shout startles Student 4 out of reverie; they sit Student 4 down in chair.)

STUDENT 5: It's time you learned about homophones and homonyms!

STUDENT 6: There are hundreds!

STUDENT 4: You're not going to show me every one? *(jumps up)*

(Students 7 and 8 push Student 4 back down in chair.)

STUDENT 7: As many as it takes!

STUDENT 8: As long it takes!

STUDENT 1: Let the homophones begin!

STUDENT 2: "The horse is hoarse from shouting!"

STUDENT 3: What are the homphones?

STUDENT 4: Uhhhhh. . .

STUDENT 5: *(writes "horse" on board)* The horse — H-O-R-S-E —

STUDENT 6: *(writes "hoarse" on board)* Is hoarse — H-O-A-R-S-E — from shouting.

STUDENT 4: Well, of course, the horse is hoarse! It's been shouting!

STUDENT 2: Try this one: "The queen was seen at the scene."

STUDENT 4: *(concentrates, squints, flexes fists)* "Seen" — spelled S-E-E-N. . .

STUDENT 5: Correct! *(writes "seen" on board)*

STUDENT 4: *(concentrates, squints, flexes fists)* Annnnnndddd "scene" — spelled S-C-E-N-E. . .

STUDENT 6: Correct! *(writes "scene" on board)*

STUDENT 4: That wasn't so hard after all! Homonyms, shmomonyms!

STUDENT 1: Not so fast! Let's see how you stack up in real competition!

(Students 1, 2, 3 group together to left of chalkboard; Students 4, 7, 8 group together to right of chalkboard.)

STUDENT 1: We're Red Team!

STUDENT 8: We're Blue Team!

STUDENT 5: A sentence will be written on the board, and the words that are homophones or homonyms will be missing.

STUDENT 6: The first team to fill in all the missing words wins that round.

STUDENT 5: But only if they spell the missing words correctly. Ready, Red Team?

STUDENTS 1, 2, 3: Ready!

STUDENT 6: Ready, Blue Team?

STUDENTS 4, 7, 8: Ready!

(Student 5 writes: "After the shoemaker ___ the shoes, he ___ them."; Teams murmur among themselves.)

STUDENT 1: After the shoemaker soled the shoes, he sold them.

STUDENT 5: Homophones are correct. Now spell them!

STUDENT 1: After the shoemaker S-O-L-E-D the shoes, he S-O-L-D them.

(Student 5 writes "soled" and "sold" in the blanks.)

STUDENT 6: Red Team wins round one!

(Student 6 writes: "There are a ___ of ___ trees in the yard."; Teams murmur among themselves.)

STUDENT 4: There are a pair of pear trees in the yard.

STUDENT 6: Homophones are correct. Now spell them!

STUDENT 4: There are a P-A-I-R of P-E-A-R trees in the yard.

(Student 6 writes: "pair" and "pear" in the blanks.)

STUDENT 5: Blue Team wins round two!

(Student 5 writes: "Tom was looking ___ a clover with ___ leaves."; Teams murmur among themselves.)

STUDENT 7: "For" and "four!" Tom was looking for a clover with four leaves.
STUDENT 5: Homophones are correct. Now spell them!
STUDENT 7: Tom was looking F-O-R a clover with F-O-U-R leaves.

(Student 5 writes "for" and "four" in the blanks.)

STUDENT 6: Blue Team wins round three!

(Student 6 writes: "Mary left ___ class an ___ after the last bell."; Teams murmur among themselves.)

STUDENT 2: The homophones are "our" and "hour." Mary left our class an hour after the last bell.
STUDENT 6: Homophones are correct. Now spell them!
STUDENT 2: Mary left O-U-R class an H-O-U-R after the last bell.

(Student 6 writes: "our" and "hour" in the blanks.)

STUDENT 5: Red Team wins round four! Score tied two-all!
STUDENT 6: And now we move up to Extreme Homophone Challenge! Three in a sentence!

(Team Members groan as Student 5 writes: "Alice said, 'When I get married, ___ walk down the ___ on the beautiful ___ of Hawaii.'"; Teams murmur among themselves.)

STUDENT 8: I know! I'll, aisle, isle!
STUDENT 5: Full sentence, please!

STUDENT 8: "Alice said, 'When I get married, I'll walk down the aisle on the beautiful isle of Hawaii.'"

STUDENT 5: Homophones are correct. Now spell them!

STUDENT 8: "Alice said, 'When I get married, I-apostrophe-L-L walk down the A-I-S-L-E on the beautiful I-S-L-E of Hawaii.'"

(Student 5 writes: "I'll," "aisle" and "isle" in the blanks.)

STUDENT 6: Blue Team wins round five and lead three rounds to two!

(Student 6 writes: " ___ waiting for ___ parents over ___."; Teams murmur among themselves.)

STUDENT 3: The homophones are "they're," "their" and "there." They're waiting for their parents over there.

STUDENT 6: Homophones are correct. Now spell them!

STUDENT 3: T-H-E-Y-apostrophe-R-E waiting for T-H-E-I-R parents over T-H-E-R-E.

(Student 6 writes: "they're," "their" and "there" in the blanks.)

STUDENT 5: Red Team wins round six, and the score is tied!

STUDENT 6: Should we have a tie-breaker?

STUDENT 2: *(indicating audience)* Let's have the whole class compete!

STUDENT 6: That's a great idea! They can come up with new sentences for us to practice.

STUDENT 3: Maybe even sentences with *four* homophones!

(Students gasp and recoil in awe; Student 4 starts to exit right.)

STUDENT 1: *(to Student 4)* Say, where are you off to?

STUDENT 4: The hardware store. My mother told me to get a couple of yolks for dinner.

STUDENT 1: Wait a minute. Your mother wants you to get a large wooden frame to join the heads of two farm animals? That's the kind of yoke — Y-O-K-E — you get in a hardware store! Don't you mean yolk spelled Y-O-L-K, as in the yellow part of an egg?

STUDENT 4: No, we're having my cousins — the McSlobs — over. Their dinner manners are so bad, we have to put a Y-O-K-E over them so they don't eat everything on the table! *(pause)* Just yoking!

STUDENT 2: *(to audience)* Here's one last homonym for you!

STUDENT 3: *(to audience)* Time flies like an arrow—

STUDENTS 5: *(to audience)* But fruit flies like bananas!

STUDENTS 1-8: *(to audience)* Ta-da!

(LIGHTS OUT)

THE END

mathematics

THE METRIC SYSTEM RULES!
(Basic Math)

Basic Concept:

This play introduces *the metric system*, defining basic units of measurement in *length*, *mass*, *volume*, *area* and *temperature*, along with providing *conversion formulas*.

Pre- or Post-Play Activities:

• Have students contact the U.S. Metric Association, Inc., a national non-profit organization founded in 1916, which advocates U.S. conversion to the modern metric system. Address: 10245 Andasol Avenue, Northridge CA 91325-1504. Web site: **http://lamar.colostate.edu/~hillger/**.

• Have students make a centimeter ruler and use it to measure objects around the classroom.

• Have students take a weather map from a daily newspaper and translate Fahrenheit temperatures into Celsius and then vice versa, from Celsius to Fahrenheit.

Discussion Questions:

• According to recent legislation, by Dec. 31, 2009 all products sold in Europe will be required to have only metric units on their labels. Why do you think European countries have been a leader in the move to metric?

• Consult an encyclopedia and find out what other measurement systems have been used over the centuries. Why did these systems not gain widespread acceptance? Why do you think the metric system has become the international standard?

STAGE SET: a classroom; at mid-center are a medium-size table and a chalkboard

CAST: 8 actors, min. 3 boys (•), 5 girls (+)

+	Gretchen	+	Shelley
•	Parker	•	Ang
•	Andrew	+	Jody
+	Gabrielle	+	Bettina

PROPS: chalk; chalkboard eraser; large ruler; juice bottle

COSTUMES: characters wear contemporary school clothes

(LIGHTS UP FULL ON SHELLEY entering from left and crossing to table at center; she is dressed in bulky winter clothes and begins taking off her hat, coat, mittens and boots as soon as she gets to the table.)

SHELLEY: Gee whiz, it's really hot in here! And my mother *almost* made me wear long johns today! I'd be melted to a puddle!

(GRETCHEN enters from right, dressed in summer clothes, and crosses to table.)

SHELLEY: Hi, Gretchen!

GRETCHEN: Hi, Shelley! What a beautiful spring day!

SHELLEY: Seems like the middle of summer! How did you know to dress for a sudden heat wave?

GRETCHEN: I listened to the weather forecast before I left for school. The temperature is supposed to be almost 25 degrees by noon.

SHELLEY: Excuse me? Did you say the high temperature will be 25 degrees?

GRETCHEN: Maybe even 30 degrees tomorrow. If that happens, I'm going swimming in the lake.

SHELLEY: Thirty degrees and you're going to swim outside?

GRETCHEN: Sure. When it's that hot, what else can you do?

SHELLEY: When it's 30 degrees outside, *I* put on ice skates and break out the hot chocolate. Gretchen, do you have a fever?

GRETCHEN: No, I'm using the metric, or Celsius, system of reading temperature. Take the regular Fahrenheit temperature on the thermometer and subtract 32, then divide that result by one-point-eight and you have the Celsius, or metric temperature.

SHELLEY: Oh. Why?

GRETCHEN: Because the metric system is the measuring system used by almost every country around the world.

SHELLEY: Oh. Why?

GRETCHEN: Because almost every product made in the world today uses the metric system. And in the United States, scientists use metric measurement exclusively.

SHELLEY: Oh. Why?

GRETCHEN: Because it's the 21st century, Shelley, and the metric system is the measurement system of the future.

SHELLEY: Oh. Why?

GRETCHEN: Because the metric system makes sense — and it's fun! I'll show you!

(Gretchen steps to the chalkboard and picks up the chalk; she writes the number "10" on the board.)

GRETCHEN: The metric system is based on units of 10.

SHELLEY: Like decimals?

GRETCHEN: That's right. Just like decimal system.

SHELLEY: Which is a system that uses a decimal point to show tenths and hundredths.

GRETCHEN: Correct. Also like our money system that Thomas Jefferson proposed back in the 1790s.

(Gretchen writes "100 cents = 1 dollar" on the board.)

SHELLEY: One dollar is made up of 100 cents. That's easy!

GRETCHEN: That's metric!

(PARKER, ANG and JODY enter from left and cross to center.)

SHELLEY: Hi, Parker! Hi, Ang!

GRETCHEN: Hi, Jody!

JODY: What are you doing?

GRETCHEN: We're talking about the metric system.

PARKER: Wow! The metric system is way cool!

ANG: Do you know the basic metric system prefixes?

(Ang steps to the chalkboard and picks up the chalk; he writes the letters "μ," "m," "c," "d," "k," "M" on the board.)

PARKER: The first letter, that funny-looking "u" with an extra leg hanging down the side is the symbol for "micro." A micro is a one-millionth part of something.

(Ang writes "micro = 0.000001" next to "μ.")

PARKER: So if you have something that weighs a gram, a *microgram* weighs one-millionth of a full gram.

(Ang writes "1 microgram (μg).")

SHELLEY: That's pretty light.

JODY: You bet it is. The small "m" stands for "milli." A milli is a one-thousandth part of something.

(Ang writes "milli = 0.001" next to "m.")

JODY: If you have something that weighs a gram, a *milligram* weighs one-thousandth of a full gram.

(Ang writes "1 milligram (mg).")

SHELLEY: That's getting heavier.

PARKER: The "c" stands for "centi," which stands for a one-hundredth part of something.

(Ang writes "centi = 0.01" next to "c.")

SHELLEY: And a *centigram* weighs one-hundredth of a full gram.

(Ang writes "1 centigram (cg).")

JODY: All right! Now you're catching on! The "d" stands for "deci," which stands for a one-tenth part of something.

(Ang writes "deci = 0.1" next to "d.")

SHELLEY: Which means a *decigram* weighs one-tenth of a full gram.
PARKER: Right again, and our gram is getting heavier! The "k" stands for "kilo." A kilo is one thousand times something.

(Ang writes "kilo = 1000.0" next to "k.")

SHELLEY: A *kilogram* is one thousand grams!

(Ang writes "1 kilogram (kg).")

JODY: Yes, indeed! And the capital "M" stands for "mega," which stands for one million times something.

(Ang writes "mega = 1,000,000.0" next to "M.")

SHELLEY: A *megagram* is one million grams! Huge!

(Ang writes "1 megagram (Mg).")

ANG: Those are the basic metric system prefixes. Now we can talk about the *stem unit*.
SHELLEY: What's a stem unit?

JODY: The stem unit is the object you're measuring. The stem unit we were just measuring was the gram.

GRETCHEN: When you measure weight in the metric system, the stem unit is the *gram.*

PARKER: When you measure length in the metric system, the stem unit is the *meter.*

JODY: When you measure volume in the metric system, the stem unit is the *liter.*

ANG: And when you measure area in the metric system, the stem unit is also the *meter.*

SHELLEY: Okay, I understand all that. But how do these metric units compare to, you know, units like inches and miles and pounds?

(ANDREW, GABRIELLE and BETTINA enter from right and cross to center.)

GRETCHEN: Look, it's Andrew and Gabrielle and Bettina!

ANDREW: Hi, everybody! What's up?

ANG: We need some conversion formulas for metric units.

BETTINA: Start with your basic ruler. *(holds up a ruler from the table)* On one side are measurements in inches. On the other side are measurements in centimeters.

GABRIELLE: Notice the "CM" printed on the centimeter side and the "IN" printed on the inch side.

BETTINA: *(to Shelley)* So when the ruler reads one inch, how many centimeters does it read?

SHELLEY: *(examines ruler)* It looks like two-and-a-half centimeters.

ANDREW: Close. It's actually two-point-fifty-four centimeters, which is just a little bit more than two-and-a-half.

(Ang writes "1 inch = 2.54 centimeters" on the board.)

SHELLEY: So one inch is equal to two-point-fifty-four centimeters?

BETTINA: That's right. Can you figure out how many centimeters are in two inches?

SHELLEY: I'd multiply two-point-fifty-four times two,
which would make. . .

(Ang writes "2 x 2.54 = 5.08" on the board.)

SHELLEY: A little over five centimeters?

GABRIELLE: Five-point-oh-eight centimeters to be exact.

SHELLEY: What about feet?

ANDREW: To find how many feet equal how many meters,
you multiply the number of feet times point-three-oh-
five.

(Ang writes "1 foot = .305 meters" on the board.)

SHELLEY: So it takes a little more than three meters to make
up one foot?

BETTINA: That's right. Now, how many centimeters make
up one foot?

SHELLEY: What?

GABRIELLE: You can get the answer two ways. First, how
many centimeters are in a meter?

SHELLEY: Hmmm. . .

ANDREW: Remember your basic metric prefixes. A centi is
what part of something?

SHELLEY: One hundredth!

BETTINA: That's right. So if there are one hundred centimeters in one meter—

GABRIELLE: And one foot equals point-three-oh-five
meters—

SHELLEY: You'd multiply one hundred times point-three-
oh-five.

(Ang writes "100 x .305 = 30.5" on the board.)

ANDREW: And get thirty-point-five centimeters in a foot.

PARKER: You could get the answer another way.

SHELLEY: How?

JODY: You know that there are twelve inches in a foot, right?

SHELLEY: Right?

GRETCHEN: Multiply the number of centimeters per inch—

SHELLEY: Two-point-fifty-four!

PARKER: Times twelve, the number of inches in a foot.

(Ang writes "12 x 2.54 = 30.5" on the board.)

JODY: Which gives you thirty-point-five centimeters in a foot.

SHELLEY: That's really neat! What about miles?

ANDREW: That's another easy formula. One miles equals one-point-six kilometers.

(Ang writes "1 mile = 1.6 kilometers" on the board.)

BETTINA: And what is a kilometer?

SHELLEY: A thousand meters?

GABRIELLE: You got it!

ANDREW: So how many miles is one hundred kilometers?

SHELLEY: Hmmm. . .

BETTINA: This time you'd use division instead of multiplication. Take the number of kilometers—

SHELLEY: One hundred.

BETTINA: Divide that by one-point-six — the number of miles in one kilometer.

GABRIELLE: And you get sixty-two-point-five miles.

(Ang writes "100 kilometers / 1.6 = 62.5 miles" on the board.)

SHELLEY: Gee whiz, going back and forth between metric and non-metric is easy once you know the formulas!

JODY: And you can use rough estimates. A standard-size paper clip is three centimeters long.

GRETCHEN: A decimeter is about as long as a regular band flute.

ANG: A meter is about as tall as your vacuum cleaner.

SHELLEY: What about metric weights?

JODY: That's a different set of formulas. My cat, Miss Buttermilk Marmalade, weighs thirteen pounds. How many kilograms is that?

PARKER: Divide thirteen by two-point-two — that's the formula for converting pounds to kilograms.

(Ang writes "13 pounds / 2.2 = 5.9 kilograms" on the board.)

ANDREW: And Miss Buttermilk Marmalade weighs in at five-point-nine kilograms.

JODY: She'll be happy to hear the lower number!

BETTINA: *(displays juice bottle)* This bottle has eight fluid ounces of delicious apple juice. I wonder how much that is in metric?

GABRIELLE: The formula is one fluid ounce equals thirty milliliters.

GRETCHEN: Multiply eight fluid ounces by thirty—

(Ang writes "8 ounces x 30 milliliters = 240mL" on the board.)

SHELLEY: And you get two hundred forty mLs.

(Everyone applauds.)

SHELLEY: When did the metric system start, anyway?

PARKER: A French priest named Gabriel Mouton devised the metric system around 1670, but it wasn't until almost two hundred years later that it became widespread.

ANG: About 99% of the rest of the world now uses the metric system to measure things. It's about time we join them so we don't lose out on new products and exciting scientific breakthroughs.

BETTINA: The process of changing our system of units to the metric system is called *metric transition* or *metrication*.

ANDREW: Most of our major industries have switched to the metric system. Look for the metric numbers on the package when you buy food or soft drinks.

JODY: It's a quick way to quiz yourself on conversion formulas.

SHELLEY: I guess so. But I'm still going to have trouble going for a swim when it's only 30 degrees!

(LIGHTS OUT)

THE END

FRACTIONS
(Using Math)

Basic Concept:

This play introduces *fractions* and gives examples of their everyday use, along with the concepts of *equivalent fraction* and *least common denominator*.

Pre- or Post-Play Activities:

• Have students make differently colored counters (like the circles drawn in the play); use the counters to illustrate equivalent fractions.

• Have students make fraction strips; divide and label the strips and use them to calculate and compare equivalent fractions.

Discussion Questions:

• Have students make a list of the ways in which fractions are used in their life; create fraction problems from these real-life situations . . . then dramatize them!

• Show some pieces of music and point out the various time signatures — 3/4, 4/4, 6/8, 3/2, etc. — and explain that these are fractions, too; in what ways do the numerator and denominator of a time signature operate like a mathematical fraction? Are time signatures like 3/4 and 6/8 equivalent meters? Is a tune in 2/4 meter one-half the time of a tune in 4/4 meter?

STAGE SET: a fence 9 feet wide and 4 feet high at mid center; in front of it to the right is a small table with 3 paint brushes and a marker and tape measure and 4 buckets of paint on the ground (fence can be made of light-colored cardboard and should have 18 individual planks 6 inches wide drawn in)

CAST: 8 actors, min. 3 boys (•), 5 girls (+)

- Lucian
- Cessalee
- Antoine
- Jill

+ Eva
+ Renee
+ Alma
• Troy

PROPS: 3 paint brushes; 4 paint buckets; tape measure; black marker; bag of cookies

COSTUMES: characters wear contemporary school clothes

(LIGHTS UP FULL ON LUCIAN standing at mid center in front of a fence; he stands empty-handed staring at the fence with a contemplative expression; EVA enters from left.)

EVA: Hi, Lucian! What are you doing?

LUCIAN: Oh, hi there, Eva! I'm trying to paint this fence for my Aunt Mary.

EVA: Umm, doesn't "trying" involve actually taking a brush and laying on some paint?

LUCIAN: Well, I have a problem. I'm supposed to paint one-third of the fence.

EVA: And?

LUCIAN: I don't know how much is one-third.

EVA: That *is* a problem.

(Lucian goes to fence and stretches his arms to encompass what he thinks is one-third.)

LUCIAN: I mean, is one-third this much? Or this much? Or maybe this much here?

EVA: Well, there's one sure way to find out — and that's by using fractions.

LUCIAN: Oh, I know about fractions! That's parts of something or other. Like, "fractured" or "broken." The words "fraction" and "fracture" are from the same Latin root word meaning "to break."

EVA: You may be a great language scholar, Lucian, but you've got a ways to go as a math whiz. A fraction names the equal parts of a whole. And the key word is *equal*.

(CESSALEE enters from right and crosses to center.)

EVA: Hi, Cessalee!

CESSALEE: Hi, Eva! Hi, Lucian! I'm on my way to science club. Want to come?

LUCIAN: Sorry, I can't. I have to paint one-third of this fence.

EVA: But he's not sure exactly how much one-third is.

CESSALEE: Well, just figure out the numerator and denominator.

LUCIAN: Hold on, my numer-what-did-you-call-it?

CESSALEE: *Numerator* and *denominator* — those are the two parts of a fraction.

(Cessalee picks up marker from table and writes on fence.)

CESSALEE: The numerator is the top number of a fraction. *(writes a "1")* See? And the denominator is the bottom number of a fraction. *(writes a dividing line and a "3" under it)* One-third, one over three.

LUCIAN: Great! But how do I know how much of this fence is one-third?

EVA: Easy! You measure!

(Eva takes tape measure from table and measures width of fence.)

EVA: The fence is nine feet wide.

(To the right of "1/3" Cessalee writes "9" in the denominator position and then writes "=" between the two fractions.)

CESSALEE: You know you have to paint one-third of the fence, right?

LUCIAN: Yes.

CESSALEE: *(points to 3 in denominator of 1/3 fraction)* If the fence were three feet wide, one-third of three would be—

LUCIAN: One, obviously. But the fence is nine feet wide.

CESSALEE: Which means you have to figure what the *equivalent fraction* is to one-third.

EVA: An equivalent fraction names the same proportion, except in larger or smaller numbers.

(Cessalee draws two small circles on the fence to the left of the numbers; she colors in one and leaves the other un-colored.)

CESSALEE: If we have two circles and one is colored in and the other is not, what fraction of the circles are colored in?

LUCIAN: Half of the circles are colored in. One of two.

CESSALEE: How many are not colored in?

LUCIAN: The same, one of two, or half.

(Cessalee draws two more small circles on the fence to the left of the numbers; she colors in one and leaves the other un-colored.)

CESSALEE: We now have four circles—

EVA: Two are colored in, two are not. What fraction of the circles are colored in?

LUCIAN: That would be half. Two out of the four. And the same for the non-colored circles.

EVA: Even though you have different numbers of circles, the proportion of one-half — one to two — is the same both times.

LUCIAN: Right.

(Cessalee writes "1/2 = 2/4" under the circles.)

CESSALEE: One over two and two over four—
EVA: One-half and two-fourths—
LUCIAN: Are equivalent fractions?
EVA & CESSALEE: Correct!

(Lucian goes to fence and points to "1/3 = /9.")

LUCIAN: So to figure out one-third of nine feet, we have to find what numerator belongs in this fraction?

(Cessalee writes "x" in the numerator position.)

EVA: X marks the spot!
CESSALEE: Take the larger denominator here *(points to "9")* and divide it by the smaller denominator here *(points to "3")*.
LUCIAN: Nine divided by three would equal three.

(Cessalee erases "x" and writes in "3.")

EVA: And that's your answer! Three-ninths is equal to one-third. They are equivalent fractions.
CESSALEE: And the number three is the *least common denominator*. That's the lowest number of the two denominators.
LUCIAN: Which means I have to paint a part of the fence that is three feet wide.
CESSALEE: Correct!
LUCIAN: Hmmm. . .

(ANTOINE, RENEE and TROY enter from right and cross to center.)

LUCIAN: Hey, here's my work crew!
EVA: Hi, Antoine! Hi, Renee!
ANTOINE: Hi! This is my cousin, Troy.

TROY: Hi, everybody! What's this I hear about work? I thought there was going to be a baseball game here today.

LUCIAN: Oh, sure, after the fence is painted. We have four colors to choose from — red, blue, green and yellow.

RENEE: Can we use more than one color?

LUCIAN: Well, Aunt Mary didn't say we couldn't!

RENEE: Great! I want blue! *(picks up a paint brush)*

ANTOINE: Red for me! *(picks up a paint brush)*

LUCIAN: What color do you want, Troy?

TROY: Let's see. Renee has a brush, and Antoine has a brush and if I have a brush, that's three brushes — what brush is left for you to paint with, Lucian?

LUCIAN: Gosh, are there only three brushes? That's okay, you guys start off, I'll catch up!

TROY: Right. *(picks up a paint brush)* Guess I'll take green.

RENEE: We'll each paint one-third of the fence.

EVA: The fence is nine feet wide. Here's a tape measure, if you want to mark off each of the three sections.

TROY: We can measure another way, too. All the planks are the same distance wide, aren't they?

EVA: Yes, each plank is six inches wide.

ANTOINE: So, we count the planks and divide the total into thirds.

RENEE: *(counts planks)* There are eighteen planks.

(Cessalee writes "1/3 = x/18" on the fence.)

TROY: We have to find the equivalent fraction.

LUCIAN: Wait, I can get this! Divide the larger denominator by the smaller denominator, and that will give you X!

RENEE: Eighteen divided by three equals six. Each one of us paints six planks, and that will be one-third of the complete fence. Is that correct?

(Cessalee erases "x" and writes in "6.")

ANTOINE: That's correct. Six-eighteenths is the equivalent fraction of one-third.

LUCIAN: All right, let's go, team! Who's first?

RENEE: I have to be back home for lunch at noon. I can come back after.

ANTOINE: I've got a cold, and I can only work for a little while at a time.

TROY: I'm waiting for that baseball game!

EVA: Looks like you'll have to work in shifts, one at a time.

CESSALEE: It's almost ten o'clock. If you paint for an hour, you can probably get finished and get home for lunch.

RENEE: How long should each of us paint?

LUCIAN: Once again, fractions control my life!

ANTOINE: There are sixty minutes in one hour, right?

(Cessalee writes "1/3 = x/60" on the fence.)

TROY: Divide sixty by three and get twenty. Each of us paints for twenty minutes.

(Cessalee erases "x" and writes in "20.")

LUCIAN: All right, team, way to go! Let's get those brushes in the buckets and boogie!

(JILL and ALMA enter from left and cross to center; Alma carries a bag of cookies.)

EVE: Look, it's Jill and Alma.

JILL & ALMA: Hi, there! What's going on?

LUCIAN: Fence-painting party! You're just in time!

ALMA: We've got a bag of cookies fresh from the bakery. Want some?

LUCIAN: It's not snack time yet.

ANTOINE: Ease up, Lucian. Workers need nourishment!

TROY: How many cookies do you have?

JILL: Lots!

ALMA: Two dozen, to be exact.

JILL: And how many people want cookies?

ALL: Me!

ALMA: Eight, to be exact.

JILL: Then we have to divide the cookies into eight equal amounts. How many cookies is that?

TROY: Get Fraction Boy to figure it out!

RENEE, ANTOINE, EVA, CESSALEE: Gooooooo, Lucian!

LUCIAN: All right, all right, calm yourselves. We'll divide the cookies then get to work, okay? *(takes marker from Cessalee and writes on fence)* Let's see. One over eight is the first fraction. Then X over twenty-four is the second.

(Lucian writes "1/8 = x/24" on the fence.)

LUCIAN: Divide twenty-four by eight and the answer is three.

(Lucian erases "x" and writes in "3.")

RENEE: Three cookies apiece! Hurray!

ALMA: Come on, everybody! Snack-time!

(Alma begins passing out cookies as everyone but Lucian flocks around.)

LUCIAN: Hold on, hold on! We've got work to do!

(He is ignored and frowns for a few moments as the others dig into the cookies.)

LUCIAN: Hey, everyone, that last fraction was wrong.

JILL: Wrong? What do you mean?

ALMA: There are twenty-four cookies and eight people. Everyone gets one-eighth of the cookies — three delicious cookies each. That's basic math.

LUCIAN: Wrong. I'm not eating *my* cookies. I'm giving my one-eighth cookie share to the first person that picks up a paint brush and finishes their third of the fence!

(Everyone except Lucian starts grabbing for brushes and buckets.)

JILL: I had that brush first!
EVA: That's my bucket!
CESSLEE: Dibs on this part of the fence!
ANTOINE: Gimme!
RENEE: Stand back!
ALMA: Those cookies have my name on them!
TROY: This is way more fun than baseball!

(Lucian observes the melee and addresses audience.)

LUCIAN: Seven people going crazy for three cookies to be the first one to finish painting my fence? I don't know what kind of fraction that is, but they're the kind of numbers I'll take any day!

(LIGHTS OUT)

THE END

science

HOW BIRDS FLY
(Life Science)

Basic Concept:

This play explores the phenomenon of *bird flight*, covering basic bird anatomy and physics of flight with particular reference to feathers, wing shape and flight pattern.

Pre- or Post-Play Activities:

- Have students build a simple bird bath for birds to help them clean feathers; place it outside the classroom window or in the school yard and schedule a short period each day to observe and catalogue what birds use the bath.

- Have students engage in a feather hunt, bringing in whatever feathers they find outside and keeping a record book of where and when they were found; then mount the feathers on construction paper or cardboard and identify them using a field guide to birds.

- Invite a spokesperson from your local Audubon Club or pet store to talk about birds. An *ornithologist* is a person who studies birds; perhaps a local college or zoo has an ornithologist on staff who can take you to a zoo or aviary and explain more things about birds.

Discussion Questions:

- The early inventors who designed the first airplanes studied how birds were built and how they flew; how do you think inventors were influenced in their designs?

- Examine the design for a modern jet airplane and compare it to the physical structure of a bird. What are the similarities? What are the differences?

- Why do you think there are so many different types of birds? And why so many sizes and colors of birds? Do you think the environment where a bird lives plays an important role in its shape and color? How?

STAGE SET: a classroom with a medium-size study table at down right; glue, scissors, construction paper, needle and thread are on the table

CAST: 6 actors, min. 3 boys (•), 3 girls (+)

• Keith	+ Chenille
• Kenan	+ Agnes
• Jose	+ Eileen

EFFECT: sound — loud buzzing

PROPS: science books; tape recorder; Figures 1 and 2 made from construction paper or cardboard and black ink marker; large illustration or photo of a bird showing basic anatomy; 5 large bird feathers; 12-inch x 3-inch strip of light constuction paper

COSTUMES: characters wear contemporary school clothes; Keith is dressed as a quasi-bird superhero — a hat resembling a beak, leggings resembling feathers made from brightly-colored, rainbow-hued paper strips, upturned sneakers, large cardboard wings wrapped in tin foil attached to his arms with masking tape, rubber bands, string

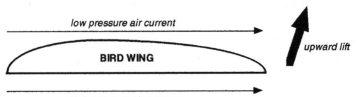

low pressure air current

BIRD WING

upward lift

high pressure air current

Fig. 2: air flow of bird in flight

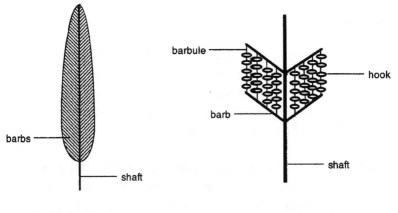

barbs

shaft

barbule

hook

barb

shaft

**Fig. 1A: bird feather,
overview**

**Fig. 1B: bird feather,
closeup**

(LIGHTS UP FULL ON AGNES and KENAN sitting at a table at down right and studying from science books. SOUND: Buzzing as if from an airplane motor; begins moderate, then grows louder. Agnes looks up and around.)

AGNES: Kenan. Do you hear that noise?

(Kenan is deep in study and doesn't respond.)

AGNES: Kenan!

KENAN: What!

AGNES: That noise! Do you hear it?

KENAN: Like some kind of buzzing?

AGNES: Yes!

KENAN: *(listens, shrugs)* It's just a truck out on the highway. Agnes, I think you're studying too hard. Maybe you should—

(SOUND: Noise grows very loud and reaches an apex as KEITH bursts in from left; he wears an absurd bird costume [large cardboard wings wrapped in tin foil attached to his arms with masking tape, rubber bands, string, etc.] and spins around the stage for several seconds before halting at down center. He switches off a small tape recorder on his belt and the buzzing noise stops.)

KEITH: It's a bird! It's a plane! It's Super-Keith!

(Keith waits for response from Agnes and Kenan, who stare at him blankly.)

AGNES: Keith, you've been eating wayyyy too much sugar lately.

KENAN: Man, we're your friends. If you were planning on doing anything crazy, you'd tell us, wouldn't you?

KEITH: Crazy? I'm just going to fly! What's crazy about that?

AGNES: Well, for starters, you're not a bird *or* a plane.

KEITH: But I've got awesome wings! Check these out! My older brother helped me make them!

(Agnes and Kenan circle around Keith, looking over his wings.)

KENAN: Uh-huh. Your older brother who helped build your submarine — out of concrete?

(JOSE, CHENILLE and EILEEN enter from left.)

JOSE: There he is! I told you he was going to fly!

KEITH: Hey, Jose!

JOSE: These are my friends Chenille and Eileen. They didn't believe me when I told them I knew the one and only Super-Keith!

CHENILLE: You're going to try to fly dressed like that?

EILEEN: Hope you have lots of life insurance!

KEITH: Why is everybody so skeptical? Birds fly; birds have wings. *(flourishes his wings) I* have wings; *I* will fly.

AGNES: There's a bit more to it than that, Keith.

KEITH: Really? Please enlighten me, professor, with *your* knowledge of birds!

AGNES: Well, first of all — what exactly is a bird?

CHENILLE: Birds are warm-blooded animals.

KEITH: Like mammals?

CHENILLE: Yes, but they lay eggs like reptiles and amphibians.

EILEEN: And there are a lot of birds. More than one hundred billion birds on earth and more than eighty-six hundred different species.

JOSE: But, even though they vary greatly in color and size, all birds have the same basic physical structure. Check this illustration!

(From behind the table, Jose raises a large illustration or photo of a bird showing its basic anatomy; Students point to the illustration as they state the bird's physical characteristics.)

KENAN: All birds have a crown.

AGNES: They have a beak or bill — but no teeth.

KEITH: How do they chew?

JOSE: They chew with a gizzard, an internal organ with muscles that crushes food.

CHENILLE: Birds have a nape— here in back.

EILEEN: And a throat — here in front.

KENAN: This is the bird's breast

AGNES: And its belly

JOSE: Back.

CHENILLE: Wing.

EILEEN: Rump.

KENAN: Flank.

AGNES: Tail.

JOSE: And feet with claws and toes.

CHENILLE: Some birds have feet especially suited for perching on branches.

(If desired, photos of the following birds can be hung around the stage and the Students can point to them as they are mentioned.)

EILEEN: Finches and robins.

KENAN: Others have feet designed for swimming.

AGNES Ducks and geese.

JOSE: Jacanas and ibises have feet that allow them to wade in water. They can walk on leaves and not sink!

CHENILLE: Woodpeckers have feet that help them climb trees.

EILEEN: Owls have feet for grabbing prey right off the ground!

KENAN: Osprey have feet that can pluck a fish right out of the water!

AGNES: But the most important thing about a bird is its—

JOSE: F—

CHENILLE: E—

EILEEN: A—

KENAN: T—

AGNES: H—

JOSE: E—

CHENILLE: R—

EILEEN: S!

ALL EXCEPT KEITH: Feathers!

(Kenan, Agnes, Jose, Chenille and Eileen each hold up a feather and wave it.)

KEITH: What's the big deal about feathers?

(Kenan, Agnes, Jose, Chenille and Eileen march around Keith and tap him with their feather as they deliver their line.)

KENAN: Birds are the only animals on Earth who have feathers.

AGNES: Feathers cover most of the bird's body except its beak and legs and feet.

JOSE: They protect the bird's body. They're waterproof and keep the bird dry and warm.

CHENILLE: Sometimes feathers even help hide the bird from predators.

KEITH: What's a feather made of?

EILEEN: Feathers are made of *keratin,* the same material found in your hair and your finger nails and toenails.

KENAN: Most birds have at least one thousand feathers

AGNES: Swans have up to twenty-five thousand feathers.

(Students lay feathers on the table; from behind table, Chenille raises and displays Fig. 1A; Eileen raises and displays Fig. 1B.)

KENAN: Figure 1A shows the basic parts of a feather. Each feather has a central *shaft.* On each side of the shaft is a flat web that has hundreds of smaller shafts called *barbs.*

AGNES: Look at Figure 1B. Branching out from each barb are hundreds of even smaller shafts called *barbules.* Each barbule has hundreds of tiny hooks — so tiny you can see them only through a microscope. These hooks hold the barbules together and give the feather its shape.

JOSE: Of course, the barbs come apart all the time. So the bird has to zip them back together by drawing the feather through its beak and nibbling at the feather until the barbs close up again.

CHENILLE: This is called *preening,* and a bird may spend several hours a day preening its feathers.

EILEEN: Birds have a preening gland just above their tail. They rub oil from the gland into the feathers to water-proof them.

KEITH: Okay, that's a feather. What does it have to do with flying?

ALL EXCEPT KEITH: Everything!

KENAN: There are three types of feathers. A bird has *down feathers*—

AGNES: *Body* or *contour feathers*—

JOSE: And *flight feathers.*

CHENILLE: The down feathers are light and fluffy. They lie underneath the body feathers right next to the bird's skin and keep the bird warm.

EILEEN: The contour feathers cover the bird's body and give the bird its distinctive shape.

KENAN: And flight feathers—

KEITH: Don't tell me — they help the bird fly!

KENAN: In ways you can't even imagine! Flight feathers are on the wings and tail of a bird. They are stiff and strong, long and slender. They help the bird steer and brake.

AGNES: There are three types of flight feathers.

JOSE: The *primary* flight feathers are at the outer edge of wing. They are attached to the bird's hand bones.

CHENILLE: The *secondary* flight feathers are attached to the bird's forearm bones.

EILEEN: The *tertiary* flight feathers are attached to the upper arm bone of the bird.

KENAN: Primary flight feathers twist like propellers to help power the bird through the air.

AGNES: Secondary flight feathers lift the bird up in the air.

JOSE: And tertiary flight feathers are the inner flight feathers of a bird's wing.

CHENILLE: Each flight feather has more than one million barbules, those tiny hooks we mentioned before that keep a feather together.

EILEEN: The barbules hook around each other and keep the feather in its shape, even when the wind or rain is blowing very strong.

KEITH: Great, so I'll super-glue some feathers on my wings, and I'll be ready to go!

KENAN: Not so fast, Super-Keith! Super-glue those feathers, and you'll be super-grounded!

AGNES: Flying is more than feathers and flapping wings. Flying is all about *lift*.

(Jose takes a strip of light construction paper from the table and holds it at mouth-level in front of Keith.)

JOSE: Here's an example of lift. I'll hold this strip of paper in front. Now, blow hard across the top.

(Keith blows hard across the top of paper.)

KEITH: The paper goes up!

JOSE: That's how it works with birds. Air moving over the top of a bird's wing lifts the wing.

CHENILLE: Why? Just like the piece of paper you blew on. The air passing over the top goes faster than the air below. This difference in air speed causes the lift.

EILEEN: When a bird flaps its wings up, the flight feathers separate to let air pass through. As the wings flap down, the feathers close and push against the air, moving the bird forward.

KEITH: *(flaps his wings)* That sounds easy!

KENAN: Maybe. But you need to have curved wings.

AGNES: A bird's wing is curved on top and flatter underneath.

KEITH: Why?

JOSE: Because the curved shape creates the lift. The shape of a bird's wing is called an *airfoil.*

(From behind table, Chenille raises and displays Fig. 2.)

CHENILLE: This is a basic diagram of the airfoil shape of a bird's wing. The airfoil makes air move faster over the wing than under it. This makes lower air pressure above the wing and higher pressure below the wing, and that difference in air pressure creates lift, which — as we saw with the construction paper — makes the bird rise in the air.

KEITH: I suppose you're going to tell me an airplane wing is just like a bird's wing?

KENAN: It is. Airplane wings have the same airfoil shape.

AGNES: Let's make an airfoil and prove it!

JOSE: Let's take this strip of paper we just used and glue the opposite ends together.
(*Jose glues ends together.*)

CHENILLE: Then after the glue dries, bend the paper into an airfoil shape — curved on top, flat underneath.

(*Jose bends paper into airfoil shape.*)

EILEEN: It's an airfoil! Now mark the center of the paper and thread a needle. Then push the needle through the center mark and pull the airfoil down the thread.

(*Jose pushes needle through paper and presents thread to Keith.*)

JOSE: Hold this, please. Hold the thread really taut.
KENAN: Now, Agnes will blow against the curved part of the airfoil.

(*Agnes blows against the airfoil, which begins to rise.*)

CHENILLE: Wow! The wing is climbing up the thread!
EILEEN: Awesome!
KENAN: If that was a real bird wing, you'd be soaring!
AGNES: Birds can fly up to fifty miles an hour. Some can fly for a thousand miles at a time without stopping.
JOSE: Many birds spend much of their lives in the air. Swallows even feed in the air, catching and eating insects as they fly along.
CHENILLE: Talk about fast food!
EILEEN: As a bird flies, its flight feathers change position all the time.
KENAN: I said before that the primary feathers act like a propeller and move the bird forward, right? Well, for balance the bird moves its tail feathers up, down or to the side.

KEITH: And for steering, it tips its wings from side to side.

AGNES: That's right!

JOSE: Every bird has a different pattern of flight. Large birds like ducks and geese fly in a straight line. Smaller birds dip. A scarlet tanager bobs up and down, flapping its wings and then folding them against its body to make a dip.

CHENILLE: Some birds flap awhile then rest and coast. An albatross can glide for a long way over the ocean just by following wind currents.

EILEEN: Hawks make use of *thermals*, which are columns of warm air that buoy them up while they search for things to eat on the ground.

KEITH: Gosh, everybody, this is great stuff to know! I can hardly wait to get some real feathers, make some new wings in an airfoil shape and—

KENAN: Earth to Super-Keith! Earth to Super-Keith!

KEITH: What?

AGNES: All birds do not fly.

KEITH: But I'm a bird, I'm a plane, I'm Super-Keith!

JOSE: You may be a bird, but you may be a flightless bird. A penguin, perhaps.

CHENILLE: Or a kiwi.

EILEEN: Or an ostrich.

KENAN: Or even a dodo. Except that they've been extinct since 1800.

KEITH: Gee, that's encouraging.

AGNES: But penguins are great swimmers!

JOSE: And ostriches are one of the fastest animals on land!

CHENILLE: You can still be Super-Keith.

EILEEN: But you might have to trade in those wings for flippers.

(LIGHTS OUT)

THE END

MAGNETS ARE MAGICAL
(Physical Science)

Basic Concept:

This play introduces the basic theory of *magnets* and related terms such as *magnetic force, micromagnets, poles, lodestone* and *repulsion/attraction.*

Pre- or Post-Play Activities:

• Have students go on a scavenger hunt around the school to find an example of magnets and magnetic force.

• Have students see what classroom objects can be magnetized and which cannot. Why?

• Have students bring in a refrigerator magnet. How does each one operate? Where is the magnet located?

• A compass is divided into 32 separate sections called *points*; have students discover what the points are called, then draw a large compass with all points represented.

Discussion Questions:

• How do scientists believe migrating birds and fish use magnetism to guide their journeys?

• How does magnetism help operate a fax machine? An airplane? A compact disc player?

• If the Earth itself were not magnetic, would a compass work?

• Can the shape of a magnetic field be changed by changing the shape of a magnet? How?

STAGE SET: a classroom; three tables used for experiments

CAST: students 1–9

PROPS: on Table A — compass; tape; small cork; bowl of water; magnetized steel paper clip; on Table B — 2 bar magnets; iron nail; steel paper clip; aluminum soda can; on Table C — 3 steel paper clips; bar magnet; iron filings; sheet of paper

COSTUMES: characters wear contemporary school clothes

(LIGHTS UP FULL ON 9 STUDENTS standing onstage facing audience; STUDENTS 1–3 stand behind Table A at down left; STUDENTS 4–6 stand behind Table B at down center; STUDENTS 7–9 stand behind Table C at down right.)

STUDENT 1: Welcome to the world of magnets!

STUDENT 2: Magnets are magical!

STUDENT 3: Their magnetic force is invisible, but can cause objects many times their size to move!

STUDENT 4: Magnets are everywhere!

STUDENT 5: In your hair dryer and washing machine!

STUDENT 6: On the refrigerator!

STUDENT 7: Elevators and golf carts!

STUDENT 8: Electric can openers and radios!

STUDENT 9: Computers and microphones!

STUDENT 1: Automobiles and vacuum cleaners!

STUDENT 2: Telephones and tape players!

STUDENT 3: Cranes and robots!

STUDENT 4: Don't forget the space shuttle!

STUDENT 5: And almost every cool toy you've ever seen!

STUDENT 6: So, what is a magnet?

STUDENT 7: A magnet is an object with the ability to attract another object—

STUDENT 8: And produce a magnetic field.

STUDENT 9: Come take a look! We'll show you a magnet in action!

STUDENT 7: *(holds up paper clip)* Here is an ordinary steel paper clip.

STUDENT 8: *(holds up bar magnet)* Here is an ordinary magnet.

STUDENT 9: Watch what happens when the magnet meets the clip.

(Student 7 moves paper clip closer toward magnet until it attaches.)

STUDENT 7: Wow! The clip sticks to the magnet!

STUDENT 8: That's awesome!

STUDENT 9: That's magnetic force! Let's see how strong that magnetic force really is!

STUDENT 7: I'll add a second paper clip to the end of the first.

(Student 7 moves a second paper clip toward the magnetized clip until it attaches.)

STUDENT 8: The second clip is hanging onto the first!

STUDENT 9: The magnetic force from the magnet has passed through the first paper clip to the second!

STUDENT 7: I'll add a third clip!

(Student 7 moves a third paper clip toward the second magnetized clip until it attaches.)

STUDENT 8: The third clip is hanging onto the second! We've got a paper clip chain!

STUDENT 9: The magnetic force from this magnet is pretty strong. It's holding three paper clips together and could probably hold several more.

STUDENT 6: So, what do we know about magnets so far?

STUDENT 5: They pull things to themselves by an invisible force called magnetism.

STUDENT 6: Can any object be a magnet?

STUDENT 4: No. Magnets are made of iron or another metal that has a lot of iron in it, like steel or cobalt or nickel.

STUDENT 5: They can be any shape or any size.

STUDENT 6: What's inside a magnet?

STUDENT 4: Micromagnets.

STUDENT 6: Micromagnets?

STUDENT 5: Millions of micromagnets.

STUDENT 6: What's inside a micromagnet?

STUDENT 4: Atoms. Like everything else in the world, magnets are made of atoms.

STUDENT 5: Atoms are always spinning around — like a ball on top of your finger.

STUDENT 6: Do they spin in any special pattern?

STUDENT 4: Not usually. But when they *do* line up and point in the same direction, they make a micromagnet—

STUDENT 5: And those millions of micromagnets make a magnet.

(Student 4 displays a bar magnet.)

STUDENT 4: And every magnet has two areas where the pull of the magnet is the strongest.

STUDENT 5: These two areas are called "poles." They have a lot of magnetic force.

(Student 5 displays a second bar magnet.)

STUDENT 5: The poles of a magnet are called "north" and "south." Watch what happens when you put two north poles together.

(Students 4 and 5 put their magnets on the table, north poles facing; they move the poles closer together.)

STUDENT 6: Whoa! The magnets are pushing each other away!

STUDENT 4: That's called "repulsion," which is the opposite of "attraction." Watch what happens when you put two different poles together — a north pole and a south pole.

(Students 4 and 5 put their magnets on the table, north pole and south pole facing; they move the poles closer together.)

STUDENT 6: The magnets are pulled toward each other!

STUDENT 5: That's attraction.

STUDENT 6: Can we make a magnet?

STUDENT 4: Sure! Take this iron nail and stroke it from one end to the other with this magnet — about fifty times and always in the same direction.

(Student 6 strokes nail with magnet.)

STUDENT 5: While you're doing that, does anyone know who discovered magnets?

STUDENT 1: There is a legend from ancient Greece that says about three thousand years ago, outside a village called Magnesia, a shepherd was tending his flock of sheep.

STUDENT 2: Magnesia was in Asia Minor, which is in the modern country of Turkey.

STUDENT 3: The shepherd had a metal crook. Suddenly, it stuck fast to a large rock!

STUDENT 1: The rock was a "lodestone" — a magnetic stone that contains a large amount of iron.

STUDENT 2: The Greeks named these stones "magnets" after the place where the shepherd had found the lodestone.

STUDENT 3: *(to Student 6)* Have you got that new magnet ready?

STUDENT 6: Almost! Forty-seven, forty-eight, forty-nine and fifty!

STUDENT 4: There! The nail should be fully magnetized.

STUDENT 5: We'll take this steel paper clip and move it toward the nail.

(Student 5 moves paper clip closer toward nail until it attaches.)

STUDENT 6: We have a magnet!

STUDENT 4: Let's see if it can pick up this soda can.

(Student 4 places a soda can below the magnetized nail; it does not attach.)

STUDENT 5: The magnet won't attract the soda can. Do you know why?

STUDENT 6: Because it's a cheap brand of soda?

STUDENT 4: No! Because the can is made of aluminum and not iron, and the magnet won't attract aluminum.

STUDENT 5: In fact, that's why magnets are used in facto-
ries that recycle metal. A magnet can tell which pieces of
metal contain iron and which don't.

STUDENT 6: Those magnets must be awfully big.

STUDENT 7: They are, but do you know what the biggest
magnet is?

STUDENT 8: You're standing on it! It's the Earth!

STUDENT 9: The Earth's core is magnetic, because it's filled
with iron.

STUDENT 7: And where is the greatest amount of magnetic
force in the Earth found? Who can guess?

STUDENT 6: At the North Pole and the South Pole?

STUDENT 8: Close. The North Pole and South Pole are the
places on the Earth's surface that are the furthest north
and furthest south.

STUDENT 9: But the places where the Earth's magnetic
force is strongest are called "magnetic north pole" and
"magnetic south pole." You can see that on any compass.

STUDENT 6: So when a compass points "north," how does
it know which way to point?

STUDENT 1: A little over a thousand years ago, people discovered that a thin bit of lodestone — remember that's
the rock with iron in it — would float in a bowl of water
and always point the same way, north and south.

STUDENT 2: That's because the lodestone points along the
lines of the strongest magnetic force.

STUDENT 3: Usually, the strongest magnet is the Earth itself,
so the needles point to the magnetic north and south poles.

STUDENT 1: Let's make a compass!

STUDENT 2: First, we have to make a needle.

*(Student 2 displays a magnetized straightened-out steel
paper clip.)*

STUDENT 2: This steel paper clip has already been magnetized just the way we magnetized that iron nail.

STUDENT 3: Then we tape our needle to a piece of cork.

(Student 3 tapes clip to cork.)

STUDENT 1: Then set the cork and needle in a bowl of water.

(Student 3 sets cork and needle in bowl of water.)

STUDENT 2: It's floating!
STUDENT 3: And it's swinging around in the water! It's pointing in one direction!
STUDENT 1: The paper clip is pointing north and south!
STUDENT 2: Let's compare it to a real compass.

(Student 2 displays a compass and sets in on the table next to the bowl.)

STUDENT 3: There it is! The real compass is pointing north *(Student 3 points.)* There!
STUDENT 1: And so is the compass we made!
STUDENTS 2 & 3: All right!

(All Students applaud.)

STUDENT 6: I wish magnetic force weren't invisible! It would be cool to actually see it!
STUDENT 7: You actually can! Check this out!
STUDENT 8: Each magnet has a limited area where it can repel and attract.
STUDENT 9: This area is called the "magnetic field."
STUDENT 7: We'll take this sheet of paper and place a magnet in the middle.

(Student 7 places magnet on the paper.)

STUDENT 8: Then we sprinkle a bunch of iron filings onto the paper.

(Student 8 sprinkles iron filings onto the paper.)

STUDENT 9: And we tap the paper a little.

(Student 9 taps paper.)

STUDENT 7: Look! The filings are making patterns around the magnet!

STUDENT 8: They're arranging themselves in curves and lines!

STUDENT 9: That's the magnetic field! The filings cluster to wherever the magnetic force is strongest.

STUDENT 1: Those are just a few things we know about magnets.

STUDENT 2: Magnetism is one of the most powerful natural forces in our world.

STUDENT 3: Birds, fish and other animals who migrate use magnetism to guide their journeys.

STUDENT 4: And we use the power of magnetism to harness the power of electricity.

STUDENT 5: To run medical scanners and airplanes.

STUDENT 6: Ships and fax machines.

STUDENT 7: CD players and power plants.

STUDENT 8: Magnets are everywhere!

STUDENT 9: Magnets are magical!

(LIGHTS OUT)

THE END

*TS UP FULL ON ABBY and LI-CHING sitting
nch at mid center, making desultory attempts to
rom a science book; sitting at a table at down
WINSLOW, who sits absolutely motionless, star-
space.)*

at's our next chapter in science?
: I don't know. Something about energy, I think.
hs) Whatever.

ng flips a few pages; Abby idly glances at Winslow.)

l you look at that!
: Look at who? Winslow?
, Winslow. Look at him!
: Why? He hasn't moved in fifteen minutes.
ctly! He just sits there, like a statue. He doesn't
muscle!
: Just call him "Mr. Energy"!

*and Li-Ching laugh; Winslow remains motionless;
R and NIAMH enter from left and cross to center.)*

Hi, Abby, Li-Ching! What's so funny?
, hi, Javier, Niamh! Look at Winslow! It's hilari-

He's not doing anything.
G: Duhhh! He's been sitting there without moving
e, ever!
e call him "Mr. Energy"!
Actually, it looks like he has lots of energy.
e you kidding? He's completely immobile!
He doesn't have *kinetic* energy, but he does have
of *potential* energy.
G: Uh-oh, runaway science terms on the loose! Red
Red alert!

SOURCES OF ENERGY
(Earth Science)

Basic Concept:

This play introduces the concept of *energy storage and transfer*, along with terms including *potential and kinetic energy*, *thermal energy*, *solar energy*, *radiation*, *conduction* and *convection*.

Pre- or Post-Play Activities:

• Have students do an experiment with thermal energy. Pour equal amounts of hot, cold and room-temperature water into three transparent glasses. With a dropper, put one drop of food coloring into the center of each glass. Wait two minutes and record how quickly the food coloring has spread through each of the glasses. In what water temperature did the coloring spread fastest? In what water temperature did the coloring spread slowest? What does this suggest about the effect of temperature on energy transfer?

• Take two rubber balls and heat or chill one of them to make each ball a different temperature. Then have students drop each ball onto a hard floor from the same height; which ball bounces higher? Why do you think this happens?

Discussion Questions:

• Energy moving through the food chain is a kind of natural "recycling" that resembles the way a used plastic bottle is recycled into a new product. What happens when the food chain process is interrupted? Draw a chart similar to Fig. 1 that shows the relationships between energy sources in an ecosystem. Talk about what might happen when links in the process are removed.

- Have students tell what they ate for lunch and trace the energy flow back through the food chain from the food item to its origin in nature.

STAGE SET: a classroom — at mid-center is a bench and a chalkboard to the left of the table; at down right is a small metal table and chair

*** UPSTAGE ***

Right   Center   Left

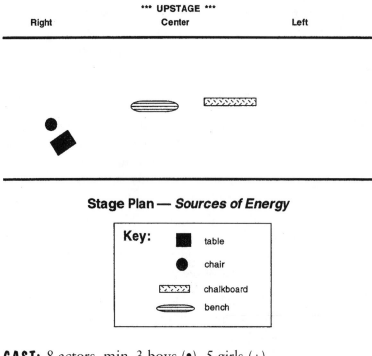

Stage Plan — *Sources of Energy*

Key:
- ■ table
- ● chair
- ▨ chalkboard
- ⬭ bench

CAST: 8 actors, min. 3 boys (•), 5 girls (+)

- + Abby
- • Winslow
- + Niamh
- + Elka
- + Li-Ching
- • Javier
- + Chandra
- • Todd

PROPS: science book; ballpoint pen; cup of ice water; refrigerator magnet; chalk

COSTUMES: characters wear contemporary school clothes

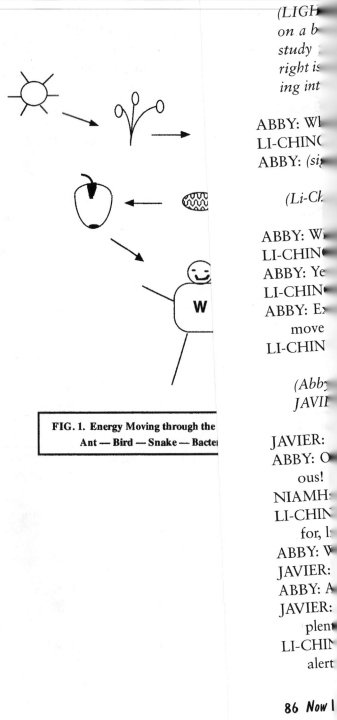

(LIGH
on a b
study
right is
ing int

ABBY: WI
LI-CHINC
ABBY: (si

(Li-Ch

ABBY: W
LI-CHIN
ABBY: Ye
LI-CHIN
ABBY: Ex
move
LI-CHIN

(Abby
JAVIE

JAVIER:
ABBY: O
ous!
NIAMH:
LI-CHIN
for, l
ABBY: W
JAVIER:
ABBY: A
JAVIER:
plen
LI-CHIN
alert

FIG. 1. Energy Moving through the
Ant — Bird — Snake — Bacter

ABBY: Wait a minute. You're saying he *doesn't* have energy, but then again, he *does*?

NIAMH: *(points left)* Do you see that car coming up the drive?

ABBY: It's slowing down to park at the curb.

NIAMH: Well, when the car is moving, that's kinetic energy — energy that comes from the motion of an object.

LI-CHING: But Winslow—

JAVIER: Look at that car again.

ABBY: The person is starting up the motor.

LI-CHING: The car is in gear, and it's pulling away from the curb.

JAVIER: While the car was parked it had potential energy.

NIAMH: Potential energy is energy that is stored in the form of a position — like an apple waiting to fall from a tree.

JAVIER: Or a condition — like a car sitting idle. Potential energy can change into kinetic energy when something happens to release the stored energy.

NIAMH: Like starting the ignition.

(Abby, Li-Ching, Javier and Niamh slowly cross to Winslow, who is still sitting motionless.)

ABBY: *(pointing to Winslow)* So *that* is actually filled with energy?

JAVIER: Chock-full to the brim!

LI-CHING: Ssshh! You might set it off!

(Abby, Li-Ching, Javier and Niamh get closer to Winslow and stare at him; Winslow suddenly moves, throwing out his left arm, which causes the others to gasp and tremble; Winslow raises his right foot and the others gasp and tremble; Winslow quickly swivels his head.)

WINSLOW: May I help you?

ABBY: He's moving!

LI-CHING: And speaking!

WINSLOW: I have no need to waste excess movement. Besides, eventually, everything comes to me. You guys did!

ABBY: He's right.

WINSLOW: I'll tell you what energy is. Energy is the ability to alter your environment. I just did that. Ergo, I *am* energy.

LI-CHING: Winslow equals energy, wow!

WINSLOW: I might not have looked busy, but I was. I've been memorizing some facts about energy.

JAVIER: Such as?

WINSLOW: Well, for a start, look around our classroom and point out the things that have energy.

(Students look around the room.)

NIAMH: *(points left)* The clock on the wall. The hands move!

ABBY: *(points right)* The aquarium in the corner. The water and the fish are moving!

JAVIER: *(points upward)* The lights are run by electricity — that's energy. And this pen has a spring in it that has potential energy.

LI-CHING: *(touches small table)* The sun has been shining on the edge of this table for the last hour. It's really warm! That's altering the environment, isn't it?

WINSLOW: It sure is. Energy can change the speed, position, direction, shape, color, composition and temperature of an object. Even a small amount of energy can lead to bigger change in energy. For example, since we've been talking, my shoelaces have loosened and now they're untied. When I get up, they'll get even more loose, and at some point my shoe will come off.

ABBY: Right when you're walking down the hall, and you stumble—

JAVIER: And crash into the science teacher—

NIAMH: Who's carrying a beaker of saline solution for an experiment—

LI-CHING: That flies into the air and splashes all over the principal coming the other direction!

WINSLOW: Who yells at me until his face turns blue and my cheeks turn red. Yep, that's a lottttttttt of energy change!

JAVIER: What happens when an object has both types of energy, potential and kinetic?

NIAMH: That's called "thermal energy." Thermal energy is the total amount of energy — potential and kinetic — of the atoms that make up an object or material.

ABBY: I thought thermal energy was another name for "heat."

WINSLOW: Heat is a kind of thermal energy, but they're not the same.

(CHANDRA, TODD and ELKA enter from left; Chandra carries a cup of ice water.)

WINSLOW: Ah-ha! A perfect example of thermal energy has just entered the room!

LI-CHING: Hi, Chandra! Hi, Todd!

ABBY: Hi, Elka!

CHANDRA, TODD & ELKA: Hi, everybody!

WINSLOW: Chandra, will you kindly assist us in this experiment?

CHANDRA: Sure! What do I do?

WINSLOW: Just sit down at the table and put your cup right in front of you.

(Chandra sits and places her cup in the middle of the table.)

WINSLOW: Elka, if you would hold out your hand, palm up, please.

(Elka holds out her hand.)

WINSLOW: Excuse my fingers.

(Winslow takes an ice cube from the cup and puts it into Elka's hand.)

ELKA: Yow! Cold!

WINSLOW: Okay, what's happening here?

CHANDRA: Elka's hand is getting frostbite!

TODD: The ice cube is melting because it came in contact with a warmer surface — Elka's hand.

NIAMH: The thermal energy from Elka's hand is transferring to the ice cube.

WINSLOW: That transfer is called "heat," when thermal energy goes from a warmer object to a cooler object.

ELKA: I think our experiment is over. *(holds up her hand)* The cube just melted.

LI-CHING: And the part of this table that's had the sun shining on it — that's an example of thermal energy, too, isn't it?

WINSLOW: It sure is. The edge of the table is the same material as the rest of the table, but the thermal energy of the sun has made it warmer.

CHANDRA: That's solar energy!

JAVIER: It's also thermal energy occurring by *radiation*. Radiation is energy that moves by waves in all directions from its source, in this case the sun shining on the table.

NIAMH: Then there's *conduction*. Conduction is when energy travels from faster-moving molecules to slower-moving molecules, like when your bowling ball hits one pin and sends it spinning into another pin.

TODD: And then there's *convection*. That's when thermal energy happens as molecules move from one place to another in a liquid or gas. It's the type of energy that produces weather.

ABBY: So the sun is a source of energy? That's called solar energy, isn't it?

WINSLOW: You bet. If you gather enough solar energy you can make it into electrical energy and provide heat and light and even power for automobiles.

LI-CHING: And when you see a windmill turning or a water wheel moving — those are examples of convection, right?

NIAMH: Yes, because the thermal energy that makes them move comes from a gas or a liquid.

(Javier takes a refrigerator magnet from his pocket and attaches it to the metal table.)

JAVIER: And this magnet I just stuck to the table — that's an example of conduction, because the molecules of the magnet have been transferred by magnetic force to the table.

ABBY: All this talk about energy is making me hungry. Is it time for lunch yet?

LI-CHING: You're always thinking about eating!

WINSLOW: That's because Abby is a prime example of another type of energy transfer — energy passing through the food chain.

ABBY: I resemble that remark!

ELKA: What do you mean, Winslow?

WINSLOW: One form of energy creates and sustains another.

TODD: How does it work?

WINSLOW: Well, it's kind of complicated—

CHANDRA: I've got an idea. Let's learn about it with a skit!

ELKA, JAVIER, NIAMH, TODD & LI-CHING: Yeh! A skit! Let's do a skit!

(Chandra crosses to chalkboard, picks up a piece of chalk and begins drawing Fig. 1 on board; other students

stand in line across stage from left to right, facing audience, starting with Elka at down left, then Javier, Niamh, Todd, Li-Ching, Abby and finally, next to the table, Winslow.)

CHANDRA: "Energy in the Food Chain," an original eco-drama by Oakdale Elementary School Science Class.

ELKA: I am the Sun. My heat and light radiates to the Earth where it shines upon all forms of plant and animal life.

(Elka mimes radiating her energy to Javier, who "absorbs" it.)

JAVIER: I am a leaf on a rose bush. I take the Sun's thermal energy and create food through photosynthesis.

(Niamh turns to Javier and mimes nibbling him; Javier kneels.)

NIAMH: I am an ant. When I chew on the plant leaf, I receive energy.

(Todd flaps his arms and mimes pecking at Niamh; Niamh kneels.)

TODD: I am a hummingbird who eats several hundred insects a day.

(Abby slithers to Todd and mimes biting his arm; Todd kneels.)

LI-CHING: I am a snake, and, my, that bird was tasty!

(Abby turns to Li-Ching and spreads her arms wide; Abby kneels.)

ABBY: I am the microscopic bacteria that feeds upon the snake when it dies. I enrich the soil and form nutrients that absorb water and energy from the Sun to grow into plants — like an apple tree.

(Abby takes an apple from her pocket and displays it; Winslow plucks the apple from her hand.)

WINSLOW: And I, Exalted Human Who Rules at the Top of the Food Chain, eat the apple! *(takes a bite from apple)*
ABBY: Hey, that's my lunch!
WINSLOW: I'm sorry! If you're going to survive in *this* food chain, you're going to have to be a lot more kinetic!

(Everyone laughs. LIGHTS OUT.)

THE END

social studies

TIME ZONES
(Geography)

Basic Concept:

This play introduces *international time zones*, along with concepts of *longitude, latitude, Greenwich Mean Time, International Date Line* and *absolute location.*

Pre- or Post-Play Activities:

• Using a map, have students discern the absolute location of their town and some towns of their relatives.

• Mark off sections of the floor and have students stand in them; then have other students calculate their time zones relative to each other.

• Have students divide into teams and find latitude-longitude coordinates of various world cities; then find their time zones.

Discussion Questions:

• Not all states or countries observe Daylight Saving Time. How did it come into being? Do you think it is needed today?

• Have students calculate what time it is in various world cities in reference to your current time. If you are in school right now, in what countries of the world are children having supper? In what parts of the world are children sleeping?

STAGE SET: a classroom; at mid-center stands a medium-size table, 2 chairs, a chalkboard

CAST: 6 actors, min. 2 boys (•), 4 girls (+)

- • Marshall   + Silvia
- + Tenicia   + Corinne
- + Bridget   • Pavan

PROPS: geography book; chalk; lunch bag; milk carton with straw; orange; black marker; flat hanging world map with time zones shown

COSTUMES: characters wear contemporary school clothes

(LIGHTS UP FULL ON TENICIA and BRIDGET sitting at the table; Tenicia is reading from a geography book, Bridget has a lunch bag and is sipping from a milk carton. MARSHALL enters from left, peering anxiously around, scratching his head and looking puzzled as he approaches the girls.)

MARSHALL: Tenicia! Bridget!

TENICIA: Hi, Marshall!

MARSHALL: Quick! Where am I?

TENICIA: What?

MARSHALL: Where am I?

BRIDGET: You're in the geography classroom. Which is where *we're* studying for *our* test.

MARSHALL: No, I mean *exactly* where am I? Right here, right now, this very spot!

TENICIA: I see! Marshall wants to know his "absolute location."

MARSHALL: Absolutely!

BRIDGET: No problem. You just have to know your latitude and longitude.

MARSHALL: Easy for you to say!

(Tenicia goes to chalkboard and draws a horizontal line.)

TENICIA: This line is called a *parallel*, and it represents latitude. It runs east and west.

(Tenicia draws a vertical line bisecting the horizontal line.)

TENICIA: This line is called a *meridian*, and it represents longitude. It runs north and south.

MARSHALL: Okay, two lines crossing each other. What's your point?

TENICIA: That *is* the point! *This* precise point where the latitude and longitude lines cross marks *your* absolute location.

BRIDGET: But now Marshall needs to look at the bigger picture. Because this point could be anywhere on Earth!

MARSHALL: *(swoons)* Anywhere on Earth? I'm more lost than before!

BRIDGET: Don't have a rhinoceros! Check this out.

(Bridget takes an orange from her lunch bag and picks up a black marking pen.)

BRIDGET: This orange represents the Earth. Around the center of the Earth going east and west is an imaginary line called "the Equator." *(draws line around center of orange)* The Equator divides the Earth into two halves, or *hemispheres*. These are called the Northern Hemisphere and Southern Hemisphere.

MARSHALL: Northern is up and Southern is down, right?

BRIDGET: Right. Now, pretend the top of this orange is the North Pole. And the bottom is the South Pole. *(draws line around center of orange)* If you draw an imaginary line through the Earth from the North Pole to the South Pole, you get an Eastern Hemisphere and a Western Hemisphere. This line that divides the Earth into east and west is called the Prime Meridian.

MARSHALL: The Prime Meridian is like the Equator, except that it divides the Earth east and west and the Equator divides the Earth north and south.

BRIDGET: That's right. And the reason this is important is—

MARSHALL: So you can divide your orange into smaller, more easily digestible pieces?

TENICIA: So you can calculate your absolute location. Look up here, Marshall.

(Tenicia labels her horizontal line "Equator" and draws a series of horizontal lines above and below the Equator line.)

TENICIA: This center line here we'll call the Equator. The lines I'm drawing above and below it are latitude lines.

MARSHALL: Parallels!

TENICIA: Got it. Now on the map, each latitude parallel represents a distance of about 69 miles. This is the first parallel. This is the second and so on.

MARSHALL: And the parallels go all the way to the North and South Poles.

TENICIA: The 90th parallel north is at the North Pole and the 90th parallel south is at the South Pole.

BRIDGET: The distance between parallels is measured in *degrees*, starting from the Equator. The Equator is at zero degrees. Which means the North and South Poles are at—

MARSHALL: 90 degrees.

BRIDGET: Correct! And it's the same for longitude lines—

MARSHALL: Meridians.

BRIDGET: Which are also approximately 69 miles apart when represented on a map.

(Tenicia labels her vertical line "Prime Meridian" and draws a series of vertical lines to the right and left.)

TENICIA: So there you are! Latitude and longitude, which together form a *grid system* for finding absolute location.

(Bridget goes to world map hanging on wall.)

BRIDGET: If you were standing at a latitude of approximately 30 degrees north and a longitude of 94 degrees west, where would you be?

(Marshall goes to map and studies it.)

MARSHALL: Beaumont, Texas!
BRIDGET: Right! What about a latitude of approximately 30 degrees south and a longitude of 165 degrees east?

(Marshall goes to map and studies it.)

MARSHALL: I'd be swimming in the Pacific Ocean between Australia and New Zealand!
TENICIA: And that's a great place for you to be, Marshall! Now, absolute location wasn't so hard to understand, was it?
MARSHALL: No. But that doesn't solve my problem.
TENICIA: What? I thought you wanted to know *where* you are?
MARSHALL: I do. But that's because I want to know *when* I are! I mean, *am* — *when* I am!

(Tenicia and Bridget throw up their hands in frustration and sit down at the table, groaning; SILVIA, CORINNE and PAVAN enter from right and greet the others.)

SILVIA: Hey, everybody!
PAVAN: Who's ready for the test?
BRIDGET: Hi, Silvia, Pavan.
TENICIA: Hi, Corinne.
CORINNE: Let's study some more!
TENICIA: We've been trying, but Marshall here has kept us going around in circles.
MARSHALL: Degrees, actually. Listen, everyone, I had a great idea about the test. The test is set for two o'clock this afternoon, right?
SILVIA: Right.
MARSHALL: Well, what if we're not in the same time zone?
PAVAN: Huh?

MARSHALL: If it's not two o'clock, we can't take the test. We've either already taken the test or we don't have to take it until some time way in the future!

CORINNE: You're not only in a different time zone, Marshall, you're in a different universe!

PAVAN: Maybe a different species!

SILVIA: I think I understand what he's getting at. When it's time for the test, Marshall is going to declare himself in a different time zone.

CORINNE: And therefore ineligible to take the test.

PAVAN: Brilliant! But deeply flawed and possibly insane. For your devious plan to succeed, you need to understand how time zones work.

(Silvia leads Marshall to the world map.)

SILVIA: Look at the world map again. These lines show the 24 *international time zones,* one for each hour of the day.

MARSHALL: They look just like longitude meridians.

CORINNE: That's because they are. Longitude meridians are used to show time zone lines. Each zone represents 15 degrees of longitude.

PAVAN: Which is the distance the Earth rotates in one hour.

MARSHALL: Who decides what time is when? *(points to map)* Who decides when twelve o'clock is twelve o'clock here and not somewhere else?

SILVIA: Because the *base time zone* is at the Prime Meridian.

MARSHALL: Here, in England?

CORINNE: At the Royal Observatory in Greenwich, England. Since 1884, the meridian running through this little English town has been adopted throughout most of the world as the Prime Meridian and base time zone.

MARSHALL: It's zero degrees in Greenwich.

PAVAN: And whatever time it is in Greenwich is called Greenwich Mean Time or GMT.

SILVIA: Which means that if you travel 15 degrees to the east, you've traveled one hour ahead of what time it is in Greenwich.

CORINNE: If the Greenwich Mean Time or GMT in the base time zone is noon, what time is it in the next time zone to the east?

MARSHALL: One o'clock? In the afternoon?

PAVAN: Right. And if you travel 15 degrees longitude to the west, say, to Iceland—

MARSHALL: It's eleven o'clock in the morning, one hour behind Greenwich Mean Time.

BRIDGET: So just how do you think you can get out of taking the test?

TENICIA: I bet he's hoping he's on the other side of the International Date Line.

MARSHALL: The "non-test" side!

SILVIA: Well, think again. As the map shows, when you head east you eventually get to the 180th meridian—

(Marshall runs a finger along the map to the end, then back again to the 180th meridian at the other end of the map.)

MARSHALL: Which is pretty much in the middle of the Pacific Ocean!

CORINNE: This is the International Date Line, an imaginary line that runs along the 180th meridian with a couple zigzags here and there.

PAVAN: The sun has already risen on the western side of the line, and it's a new day already.

MARSHALL: *(points to map)* So, here on the eastern side of the International Date Line, it's Monday?

PAVAN: Correct.

MARSHALL: *(points to map)* And here on the western side of the International Date Line, it's Tuesday?

PAVAN: We have a winner!

TENICIA: Travelers crossing the line from east to west — from Los Angeles to Tokyo — "lose" a day.

SILVIA: Because the date is now a day ahead.

BRIDGET: But if you cross it from west to east — from Manila to Honolulu — you "gain" a day.

CORINNE: Because the date is now a day behind what you just left.

MARSHALL: *(glumly)* I see. So, we're still in the "gotta take a test today zone"?

PAVAN: I'm afraid so. But wait! You've got one more miniscule chance! All together, everyone—

TENICIA, BRIDGET, CORINNE, PAVAN, SILVIA: Daylight Saving Time!

MARSHALL: *(jumps with glee)* Yes, yes! Daylight Saving Time! Of course! What is it?

BRIDGET: Daylight Saving Time has been around a while. Benjmanin Franklin first suggested it almost as a joke back in 1784.

TENICIA: But it wasn't until World War I that Daylight Saving Time was first adopted in the United States.

SILVIA: The idea was to set clocks ahead one hour in order to have more daylight during the hours when people are awake and working.

MARSHALL: More time to work? That doesn't sound promising.

CORINNE: It's important to farmers who wanted more time to work in the fields. And for city people, the extra hour of daylight cuts down the need for artificial light in the evening hours.

PAVAN: And that helps conserve energy.

MARSHALL: Taking tests uses up way too much energy! I'm all for Daylight Saving Time! Bring it on!

BRIDGET: It's already here. Daylight Saving Time went into effect this past weekend.

MARSHALL: All right!

TENICIA: All clocks are advanced one hour in the spring and set back one hour in the fall.

MARSHALL: Okay, this is spring, so the clocks moved ahead one hour. Great!

SILVIA: Which means the test is coming one hour *earlier* than it would have last week — before Daylight Saving Time.

(Marshall gasps and clutches his throat; the others laugh.)

BRIDGET: Now do you know exatcly when and where you are, Marshall?

TENICIA: He's in a permanent state of panic!

CORINNE: I think I hear the teacher coming down the hall!

PAVAN: Either that, or the steady tick-tock, tick-tock of Destiny!

MARSHALL: Where's that International Date line when you need it? How far are we from Tokyo? Does anybody know if there's such a thing as Daylight Wasting Time?

(LIGHTS OUT)

THE END

GOVERNMENTS OF THE WORLD
(Citizenship)

Basic Concept:

This play introduces the basic types of *political systems* and, using analogy, their application to modern society.

Pre- or Post-Play Activities:

• Have students make a chart of several countries and name the system of government of each.

• Have students make a chart showing a timeline of government systems in world history, when they originated, when they were at their peak, when they declined.

Discussion Questions:

• An early form of direct democracy was used in ancient Greece in the 5th century B.C., but it was not until the creation of the United States of America in the late 1700s that democracy again began to flourish. Why do you think democracy disappeared for so long? Why do you think it returned when it did?

• Some political scientists have predicted that in the future, all nations will belong to one world government, perhaps modeled upon the United Nations. What form of government do you think would work the best for this purpose?

STAGE SET: a classroom — at mid center is a chalkboard with 6 chairs grouped on the left, 5 chairs on the right

CAST: 12 actors, min. 4 boys (•), 8 girls (+)

+ Ms. Zingaro	• Panos
+ Misty	• Rolf
+ Trinh	• Ignacio
+ Ingrid	+ Reza
• Amir	+ Kenya
+ Subbiah	+ Gail

PROPS: chalk

COSTUMES: characters wear contemporary school clothes

(LIGHTS UP FULL ON MISTY, PANOS, ROLF, TRINH, INGRID and REZA sitting in chairs to the left of the chalkboard and AMIR, KENYA, GAIL, SUBBIAH and IGNACIO sitting in chairs to the right; everyone is talking loudly and somewhat belligerently.)

MISTY: I don't agree! That makes no sense at all!
ROLF: You don't know what you're talking about!
PANOS: If you don't like it, then why don't you just—
KENYA: No way, Jose! Noooooooooo way, Jose!

(MS. ZINGARO enters from left and observes the general uproar a moment before crossing briskly to center; the Students begin to notice Ms. Zingaro's presence and come to attention.)

MS. ZINGARO: Thank you. Would someone like to tell me what this is all about?

(Ingrid raises her hand.)

INGRID: Yes, Ingrid.

(Ingrid stands.)

INGRID: We've started a club, Ms. Zingaro.
MS. ZINGARO: Really? That's wonderful. What is the name of the club?
INGRID: The Good Manners Club.
MS. ZINGARO: Indeed! I wasn't aware that good manners included everyone talking at once at the top of their lungs and not listening to their neighbor.

(Reza raises her hand; Ingrid sits.)

MS. ZINGARO: Yes, Reza.

(Reza stands.)

REZA: This is our first meeting. We're trying to select a form of government for the club, but we can't agree what kind to pick.

MS. ZINGARO: That's a very good start. Every club does need a set of laws and policies to govern the conduct of its members, and that's what a government provides for its citizens. But there are nearly two hundred nations in the world and many types of government to choose from. What are some of the suggestions you've had?

(Ignacio raises his hand; Reza sits.)

MS. ZINGARO: Ignacio.

(Ignacio stands.)

IGNACIO: One was *monarchy.*

MS. ZINGARO: Monarchy. Misty, will you please write these on the board? Thanks.

(Misty goes to chalkboard and writes the suggestions, starting with "monarchy.")

MS. ZINGARO: Who can tell us about the form of government called monarchy?

IGNACIO: I know, Ms. Zingaro. Monarchy is a form of government with a hereditary head of state, like a king or queen or other person with a royal title.

MS. ZINGARO: What does hereditary mean, Ignacio?

IGNACIO: Hereditary means having something passed down from a parent to the child, like property or a title. A king becomes a king because his father was king, and he has absolute power over everyone.

MS. ZINGARO: That's true. A couple of centuries ago most of the world's governments were monarchies, where the power to rule was passed only through the family. Now, there only a couple dozen governments that are monarchies, and in most of those, the ruler does not have absolute power. What was another suggestion?

(Amir raises his hand; Ignacio sits.)

MS. ZINGARO: Amir.

(Amir stands.)

AMIR: *Feudalism.*

MS. ZINGARO: Feudalism. What can you tell us about the form of government called feudalism, Amir?

AMIR: Feudalism was based upon landlords collecting tribute from tenants who worked their land. In return for the tribute, the landlords offered the tenants military protection.

MS. ZINGARO: Feudalism was very common throughout Europe in the Middle Ages and in many other parts of the world where most of the people earned a living by farming. Now, in the 21st century, feudalism has vanished as a form of government.

(Subbiah raises her hand; Amir sits.)

MS. ZINGARO: Subbiah.

(Subbiah stands.)

SUBBIAH: *Fascism* is a form of government in which the state and the leader are held as one and glorified almost as if the leader were a king or queen.

MS. ZINGARO: It sounds like a monarchy.

SUBBIAH: But the leader of a fascist government doesn't receive their title from their family. They might take it by force or they might even be elected.

(Gail raises her hand; Subbiah sits.)

MS. ZINGARO: Gail.

(Gail stands.)

GAIL: Sometimes a fascist government is a *militaristic government*. That's a state dominated by the military.
MS. ZINGARO: That's correct. Any other suggestions?

(Trinh raises her hand; Gail sits.)

MS. ZINGARO: Trinh.

(Trinh stands.)

TRINH: An *oligarchy* is a form of government where a small group of people rule, usually because they have more money and resources than everyone else.
MS. ZINGARO: That sounds like a modern version of feudalism, doesn't it?

(Rolf raises his hand; Trinh sits.)

MS. ZINGARO: Rolf.

(Rolf stands.)

ROLF: *Democracy* is a form of government.
MS. ZINGARO: Yes, and there are several types of democratic governments. Which did you suggest?

ROLF: I suggested *representative democracy*. That's where the people vote for other people to represent them in making laws and decisions.

MS. ZINGARO: The United States is a representative democracy, isn't it? We vote for congress people and senators and state legislators and city councilors to make laws for us. We vote for presidents and governors and mayors to help enforce the laws. Representative democracy is also referred to as a *republic*.

(Kenya raises her hand; Rolf sits.)

MS. ZINGARO: Kenya.

(Kenya stands.)

KENYA: I suggested *direct democracy*. That's where the people make the laws themselves. They vote on the laws directly.

MS. ZINGARO: Direct democracy is the purest form of democracy because each citizen qualified to vote can have a direct say in each law and policy the government makes. But it's hard to carry out when you've got millions of people over a large area all wanting to express their opinion on every decision.

(Panos raises his hand; Kenya sits.)

MS. ZINGARO: Panos.

(Panos stands.)

PANOS: What about *parliamentary democracy*? That's a system that has a parliament, or congress, elected by the people. Then the government is formed by the party that has the most members of the parliament.

MS. ZINGARO: Many nations today have turned to parliamentary democracy. But when the members of the parliament disagree with each other, that can often immediately end the government, and the people have to have another election right away.

(Reza raises her hand; Panos sits.)

MS. ZINGARO: Reza.

(Reza stands.)

REZA: *Communism* is a system of government based upon communal ownership of all property and means of production. Everyone works for everyone else, and no one owns any property of their own.

MS. ZINGARO: Probably the very first human societies had a communal form of government, where all resources and all responsibilities were shared equally in order to survive. But as society grew larger and more complex, it became difficult to get everyone in the society to agree to share equally. In the 20th century several countries including Russia and China tried to have a communist system of government, but they quickly became fascist and militaristic.

(Ingrid raises her hand; Reza sits.)

MS. ZINGARO: Ingrid.

(Ingrid stands.)

INGRID: What about *socialism*? Isn't that a type of communism?

MS. ZINGARO: Partly. A socialist government owns the main means of economic production in the nation and then redistributes the wealth through programs geared to people's special needs and income levels. Are there any other types of government?

(Misty raises her hand; Ingrid sits.)

MS. ZINGARO: Misty.
MISTY: What about no government? What about *anarchy*?

(Students chuckle.)

MS. ZINGARO: Don't laugh! There are some people who believe that the best government is no government at all.
MISTY: But then who makes the laws?
MS. ZINGARO: In an anarchy, there aren't any laws. Or any elections or representatives.
MISTY: Then how can people make decisions for the common good?
MS. ZINGARO: They don't. Because no one can agree on what the common good is. Is that all the suggestions?

(Trinh raises her hand; Misty sits.)

MS. ZINGARO: Trinh.

(Trinh stands.)

TRINH: Ms. Zingaro, we've heard the definitions of the different governments. But we don't know what they really mean to us here in school.

(Students murmur assent; Trinh sits.)

MS. ZINGARO: How about using some analogies? Amir, you have two cows. You live in a society ruled by feudalism.

What do you think that form of government would mean to you and your two cows?

(Amir stands.)

AMIR: My lord would take some milk from the cows whenever he wanted.

MS. ZINGARO: Ignacio, you have two cows and live in a monarchy. What might happen to you and your cows?

(Ignacio stands; Amir sits.)

IGNACIO: My king would take milk from the cows whenever he wanted. And cut off my head if it was sour.

(Everyone laughs; Ignacio sits.)

MS. ZINGARO: Gail, you live under a militaristic government.

(Gail stands.)

GAIL: The government takes one of my cows and drafts me into the army.

MS. ZINGARO: That's a possibility. Subbiah, you live under a fascist government.

(Subbiah stands.)

SUBBIAH: The government takes both cows and shoots me.

(Everyone laughs; Subbiah sits.)

MS. ZINGARO: We laugh, but it's often not that far from the truth. Trinh, you live in an oligarchy.

(Trinh stands.)

TRINH: The government takes both my cows and hires me to take care of them. Then, the government sells me the milk.

MS. ZINGARO: That's using your imagination. Kenya, you live in a direct democracy and have two cows.

(Kenya stands; Trinh sits.)

KENYA: My neighbors vote and decide who gets the milk.

MS. ZINGARO: Rolf, you live in a republic, or representative democracy.

(Rolf stands; Kenya sits.)

ROLF: My neighbors pick someone to tell me who gets the milk.

MS. ZINGARO: Panos, you live in a parliamentary democracy. What happens to your milk?

(Panos stands; Rolf sits.)

PANOS: My neighbors pick someone who picks somebody else to tell me who gets the milk. Then they argue, and my milk spoils.

MS. ZINGARO: Ingrid, you live in a socialist state.

(Ingrid stands; Panos sits.)

INGRID: My neighbors help me take care of my cows, but the government takes all the milk and gives me milk from someone else's cow.

MS. ZINGARO: Reza, you live in a communist state.

(Reza stands; Ingrid sits.)

REZA: My neighbors help me take care of my cows, and we all share the milk. But I can never own more than two cows.

MS. ZINGARO: And finally, Misty, you live under anarchy. There is no government at all in your society.

(Misty stands; Ingrid sits.)

MISTY: My neighbor steals my cows and tells me they were actually horned rabbits from Mars.

(Everyone laughs; Misty sits.)

MS. ZINGARO: Well, does that help you decide what form of government The Good Manners Club should have?

(Students murmur assent.)

MS. ZINGARO: And no matter which form you choose, remember what the first president of our country, George Washington, said about government: "The basis of our political system is the right of the people to make and to alter their constitutions of government."

(LIGHTS OUT)

THE END

SENECA FALLS CONVENTION, 1848 (History)

Basic Concept:

This play recreates the Seneca Falls Convention of 1848, which was the first gathering in the United States that issued a formal call to establish the legal and economic rights of women, including a constitutional amendment to give women the right to vote.

Pre- or Post-Play Activities:

- Have students do research on the background of the Convention's main issues and participants mentioned in the play. Here are some starting points:

    — The National Women's Hall of Fame
    76 Fall Street, Seneca Falls, NY 13148
    web site: **http://www.greatwomen.org**

    — Women's Rights National Historical Park
    136 Fall Street, Seneca Falls, NY 13148
    web site: **http://www.nps.gov/wori/wrnhp.htm**

    — The National Women's History Project
    7738 Bell Road, Windsor, CA 95492
    web site: **http://www.nwhp.org**

- View the PBS film *Not for Ourselves Alone: The Story of Elizabeth Cady Stanton and Susan B. Anthony*, produced by Ken Burns and Paul Barnes (web site: **http://www. pbs.org/stantonanthony**); afterwards, explore some of the reasons it took so long after the Seneca Falls Convention of 1848 for women to get the right to vote.

Discussion Questions:

- The Declaration of Rights and Sentiments adopted at the Convention used the phrase "We hold these truths to be self-evident that all men and women are created equal. . ." This is similar to the phrase that appears in the Declaration of Independence except that *and women* has been added. Why do you think the delegates at the Seneca Falls Convention thought it necessary to add *and women*? Why do you think the delegates who drafted the original Declaration of Independence said only that *all men are created equal*?

- If you are a United States citizen, you will be able to vote when you are 18 years old. Suppose you did not have this right; make a list of the ways in which your life would be affected.

- Suppose you did not have the right to vote; what peaceful methods of protest and change would you pursue to convince the government to give you the right?

STAGE SET: a short bench at down left; at mid center are a podium (or pulpit) and a small writing table flanked on either side by two long benches (or pews)

CAST: 15 actors, min. 5 boys (•), 10 girls (+)

+ Charlotte Woodward Pierce (age 91)
+ Charlotte Woodward (age 19)
+ Bridget Farrelly, Reporter
• Christopher Campbell, Reporter
+ Elizabeth Cady Stanton
+ Lucretia Mott
+ Mary Ann McClintock
• James Mott
+ Martha Wright
+ Jane Hunt

- Frederick Douglass
- 2 Male Delegates
+ 2 Female Delegates

PROPS: gavel; pen; pencil; quill pen; 1920 reporters' notebook; 2 1848 writing pads; 1848 newspaper

COSTUMES: Charlotte Woodward Pierce and Bridget Farrelly wear 1920-style clothing — long, dark dress and wide-brimmed hat (or hair pinned up in a bun); for Charlotte Woodward Pierce, a suit with mid-calf skirt and a small, round flapper hat for Bridget Farrelly; 1848 characters wear clothes from that period — women with long, dark, hoop-skirted dresses and bonnets; men with dark frock coats and stovepipe hats

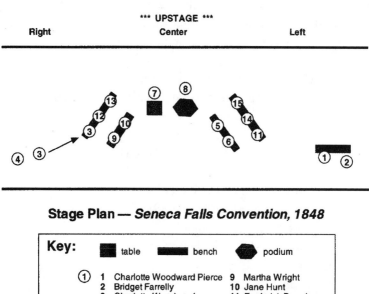

Stage Plan — *Seneca Falls Convention, 1848*

| Key: | ▮ table | ▬ bench | ⬣ podium |

①	1 Charlotte Woodward Pierce	9 Martha Wright
	2 Bridget Farrelly	10 Jane Hunt
	3 Charlotte Woodward	11 Frederick Douglass
	4 Christopher Campbell	12 Male Delegate #1
	5 Elizabeth Cady Stanton	13 Male Delegate #2
	6 Lucretia Mott	14 Female Delegate #1
	7 Mary Ann McClintock	15 Female Delegate #2
	8 James Mott	

(LIGHTS UP LEFT ON CHARLOTTE WOOD-WARD PIERCE, an elderly woman, entering slowly with aid of cane from left; she is crossing slowly to right but stops after a couple steps to rest. SPOTLIGHT DOWN RIGHT ON BRIDGET FARRELLY, a young newspaper reporter, stands at down right writing in notebook; she notices Charlotte Woodward Pierce and crosses briskly to her at down left.)

BRIDGET FARRELLY: Mrs. Pierce! Mrs. Pierce!

CHARLOTTE WOODWARD PIERCE: *(turns)* Yes?

BRIDGET FARRELLY: Are you Mrs. Charlotte Pierce? Charlotte Woodward Pierce?

CHARLOTTE WOODWARD PIERCE: I was the last time I checked! Should I be somebody else?

BRIDGET FARRELLY: My name is Bridget Farrelly, and I am a reporter for the *Philadelphia Inquirer*. I would like to interview you for my story.

CHARLOTTE WOODWARD PIERCE: Interview me? What is so special about me? I am just an ordinary 91-year-old citizen of Philadelphia out for an ordinary stroll on an ordinary autumn day.

BRIDGET FARRELLY: Mrs. Pierce, you are far too modest. And this is no ordinary day! Today — November 2, 1920 — marks the first time American women are allowed to vote in a Presidential Election, thanks to the passage of the 19th Amendment to the Constitution this past summer.

CHARLOTTE WOODWARD PIERCE: About time Congress got around to doing something useful!

BRIDGET FARRELLY: And of the nearly two hundred women who attended the first Women's Rights Convention in 1848 and demanded that vote, you are the only one still alive to enjoy that privilege.

CHARLOTTE WOODWARD PIERCE: Not a privilege! A right! *(sits on bench at down left)* We had better sit down, Miss Farrelly. There are a few gaps in your education that need to be filled in. . .

(LIGHTS FADE DOWN LEFT, FADE UP RIGHT ON CHARLOTTE WOODWARD, a young woman, standing at down right. She holds a newspaper and glances around as if unsure of where she is.)

CHARLOTTE WOODWARD PIERCE: The summer of 1848, I was nineteen years old. I lived in the small village of Waterloo, New York, not far from Seneca Falls, and worked in a glove factory to support my family. It was a dreary existence — very hard work and long hours with *very* low pay — but that summer, I knew something extraordinary was on the horizon! Why, during that one year alone, there were revolutions in France and Italy, uprisings in Vienna, Prague, Warsaw and Berlin. Less than three weeks before the convention, slavery was abolished in the Dutch West Indies. Change was in the air, and I was bound and determined to be part of it! I arrived on the second day.

(CHRISTOPHER CAMPBELL, a newspaper reporter, enters from right, holding a writing pad and a pencil. He nearly bumps into Charlotte Woodward.)

CHRISTOPHER CAMPBELL: I beg your pardon, Miss. I say, aren't you a little young to be muddling about with this flock of old maids?

CHARLOTTE WOODWARD: And well you might beg pardon! Sir, I am shocked by your tone of disrespect for these noble delegates!

CHRISTOPHER CAMPBELL: Oh, bother my tone! "Noble delegates" did you say? Ha! *(grabs her newspaper)* The following announcement — unsigned — appeared in the *Seneca County Courier* July 14: *(reads from newspaper)*

"A convention to discuss the social, civil and religious condition and rights of Woman will be held in the Wesleyan Chapel, at Seneca Falls, New York, on Wednesday and Thursday, the 19th and 20th of July current, commencing at 10 o'clock a.m." *(gives paper back to Charlotte)* Ha!

CHARLOTTE WOODWARD: For your information, *I* am a delegate to the convention.

CHRISTOPHER CAMPBELL: And you are—

CHARLOTTE WOODWARD: Miss Charlotte Woodward, of Waterloo.

CHRISTOPHER CAMPBELL: Well, Miss Woodward of Waterloo, *I* am Christopher Campbell, correspondent for the *Courier*. I have been assigned the onerous task of reporting on this affair.

CHARLOTTE WOODWARD: And what have you learned thus far, Mr. Campbell?

CHRISTOPHER CAMPBELL: I have learned that when three hundred women and women-sympathizing men gather at a Methodist church in the middle of July, the hot air is unbearable!

(ELIZABETH CADY STANTON enters from right and proceeds to mid center. LIGHTS BEGIN TO FADE UP CENTER AS DELEGATES ENTER.)

CHRISTOPHER CAMPBELL: Ah, there goes Mrs. Henry Stanton, one of the organizers.

CHARLOTTE WOODWARD: Mrs. Elizabeth Cady Stanton, if you please! She has her *own* name!

CHRISTOPHER CAMPBELL: *(laughs)* Her own name! That's rich! When a married woman gains her own name, next thing she'll be wanting is her own property! What else do you know about that Stanton woman?

CHARLOTTE WOODWARD: She is thirty-three years old and was born in Johnstown, New York. Her first cousin is the famous abolitionist Gerrit Smith. Her father was a lawyer and judge.

CHRISTOPHER CAMPBELL: Comes from solid New England stock.

CHARLOTTE WOODWARD: As a child Elizabeth was so incensed by the unjust laws she saw in her father's law books, she took a knife and cut them off the page!

CHRISTOPHER CAMPBELL: A veritable lunatic!

CHARLOTTE WOODWARD: Judge Cady explained that the only way to do away with bad laws is to work to have them changed. And that has been her mission ever since.

(LUCRETIA MOTT and JAMES MOTT enter from right and proceed to mid center.)

CHRISTOPHER CAMPBELL: That would be James Mott and his wife, *Mrs.* Lucretia Mott, of Philadephia. He is a Quaker minister.

CHARLOTTE WOODWARD: And she also is a Quaker minister, as well as an agent for the Underground Railroad.

CHRISTOPHER CAMPBELL: Women ministers! Those Quakers are a peculiar sort! They even let their women speak in public meetings.

CHARLOTTE WOODWARD: Cherokee women have long held the right to speak in public meetings. And among the Iroquois, women were allowed to vote in tribal elections.

CHRISTOPHER CAMPBELL: Fat lot of good it did them when the white man came and took their land! Here comes Mrs. Mott's younger sister, Martha Wright, another Quakeress.

(MARTHA WRIGHT enters from right and proceeds to mid center, followed by JANE HUNT and MARY ANN McCLINTOCK.)

CHARLOTTE WOODWARD: And Jane Hunt and Mary Ann McClintock.

CHRISTOPHER CAMPBELL: It was in Hunt's house that the idea for this whole convention was first conceived.

CHARLOTTE WOODWARD: And in the McClintock house that the Declaration of Sentiments was drafted.

(TWO MALE DELEGATES and TWO FEMALE DELEGATES enter from right and proceed to mid center, taking their seats at benches.)

CHRISTOPHER CAMPBELL: The delegates are a curious mix — many Quakers and Congregationalists. Some belong to that new political party, what do they call themselves?

CHARLOTTE WOODWARD: The Free Soil Party. They are vigorously opposed to slavery.

CHRISTOPHER CAMPBELL: *(laughs)* They can have all the free soil they want, as far as I'm concerned!

(FREDERICK DOUGLASS enters from right and proceeds to mid center.)

CHARLOTTE WOODWARD: And there is Frederick Douglass!

CHRISTOPHER CAMPBELL: He is the editor of the *North Star* newspaper in Rochester.

CHARLOTTE WOODWARD: And one of the most powerful speakers in the nation against slavery. In his dignified bearing and manner, he resembles an African prince!

CHRISTOPHER CAMPBELL: That's all well and good, but can someone tell me why this convention on the rights of women is being held?

CHARLOTTE WOODWARD: Because women have no rights!

CHRISTOPHER CAMPBELL: None whatsoever!

CHARLOTTE WOODWARD: A woman in the United States of America cannot in most states attend school.

CHRISTOPHER CAMPBELL: Or practice a profession such as law.

CHARLOTTE WOODWARD: Or medicine.

CHRISTOPHER CAMPBELL: Or newspaper correspondent.

CHARLOTTE WOODWARD: She cannot own property.

CHRISTOPHER CAMPBELL: Or keep whatever wages she earns.

CHARLOTTE WOODWARD: She cannot divorce an abusive husband

CHRISTOPHER CAMPBELL: Or vote for the political leaders who make the laws that govern her.

CHARLOTTE WOODWARD: Then we agree! Women have no legal rights.

CHRISTOPHER CAMPBELL: Correct. And they should continue to have none!

CHARLOTTE WOODWARD: I have no more words to waste on you, Mr. Campbell. The meeting is about to begin.

(LIGHTS UP FULL CENTER as Charlotte Woodward crosses to center and sits in rear pew; other delegates have been seated [see Stage Plan]; James Mott stands at podium; Mary Ann McClintock is seated at a table adjacent, holding a quill pen and notepad; Christopher Campbell stands, taking notes behind Charlotte Woodward. James Mott bangs a gavel on the podium.)

JAMES MOTT: Ladies and gentleman, yesterday the Declaration of Rights and Sentiments was approved, with one hundred delegates signing their names. Today, it is our task to consider the Eleven Resolutions to the Declaration offered by Mrs. Elizabeth Cady Stanton. We begin with you, Madame Secretary.

MARY ANN McCLINTOCK: *(stands)* Resolved, that such laws as conflict in any way with the true and substantial happiness of woman, are contrary to the great precept of nature, and of no validity. *(sits)*

JANE HUNT: *(stands)* Resolved, that all laws which prevent woman from occupying such a station in society as her conscience shall dictate, or which place her in a position inferior to that of man, are contrary to the great precept of nature, and therefore of no force or authority. *(sits)*

FEMALE DELEGATE #2: *(stands)* Resolved, that woman is man's equal and was intended to be so by the Creator, and the highest good of the human race demands that she should be recognized as such. *(sits)*

MARTHA WRIGHT: *(stands)* Resolved, that the women of this country ought to be enlightened in regard to the laws under which they live. *(sits)*

FEMALE DELEGATE #1: *(stands)* Resolved, that it is the duty of man to encourage woman to speak and teach, as she has an opportunity, in all religious assemblies. *(sits)*

MALE DELEGATE #2: *(stands)* Resolved, that the same amount of virtue, delicacy and refinement of behavior required of woman in the social state, should also be required of man, and the same transgressions should be visited with equal severity on both man and woman. *(sits)*

MALE DELEGATE #1: *(stands)* Resolved, that the objection of indelicacy and impropriety, which is so often brought against woman when she addresses a public audience, comes with a very ill grace from those who encourage by their attendance her appearance on the stage, in the concert or in the feats of the circus. *(sits)*

LUCRETIA MOTT: *(stands)* Resolved, that woman has too long rested satisfied in the circumscribed limits which corrupt customs and perverted application of the Scriptures have marked out for her, and that it is time she should move in the enlarged sphere which her great Creator has assigned her. *(sits)*

ELIZABETH CADY STANTON: *(stands)* Resolved, that it is the duty of the women of this country to secure to themselves their sacred right to the elective franchise. *(remains standing)*

(There is total silence, then a fervent whispering and murmuring among the delegates until James Mott bangs his gavel.)

JAMES MOTT: Ladies and gentlemen, let us proceed. There will be time for debate after the resolutions have been read in full.

(Elizabeth Cady Stanton sits.)

FREDERICK DOUGLASS: *(stands)* Resolved, that the equality of human rights results necessarily from the fact of the identity of the human race in capabilities and responsibilities. *(sits)*

CHARLOTTE WOODWARD: *(stands)* Resolved, that being invested by the Creator with the same capabilities and the same consciousness of responsibility for their exercise, it is demonstrably the right and duty of woman, equally with man, to promote every righteous cause, by every righteous means. *(sits)*

JAMES MOTT: The Resolutions have been read. Is there any discussion?

(There is whispering and murmuring among the delegates; Female Delegate #1 stands.)

FEMALE DELEGATE #1: All of the Resolutions seem to be in good order except for *(pauses)* Resolution Number Nine. *(sits)*

MARY ANN McCLINTOCK: *(reads from notebook)* Resolved, that it is the duty of the women of this country to secure to themselves their sacred right to the elective franchise.

MALE DELEGATE #1: *(stands)* The very idea is incredible!

MALE DELEGATE #2: *(stands)* Unthinkable!

MARTHA WRIGHT: *(stands)* As much as I support— in general principle — the right of women to vote, I am concerned that passing such a Resolution will endanger all our other reforms.

FEMALE DELEGATE #1: *(stands)* We will be mocked and villified!

JANE HUNT: Perhaps now is not the best time to present such a demand.

FEMALE DELEGATE #2: All our male supporters will desert us!

LUCRETIA MOTT: Lizzie, thou wilt make the convention ridiculous.

(James Mott pounds gavel.)

JAMES MOTT: Delegates, order, please! Mrs. Stanton, do you wish to speak?

ELIZABETH CADY STANTON: I do.

(Elizabeth Cady Stanton stands; the other elegates sit.)

ELIZABETH CADY STANTON: Strange as it may seem to many, we now demand our right to vote according to the declaration of the government under which we live. The pens, the tongues, the fortunes, the indomitable wills of many women are already pledged to secure this right. The right to vote is ours. Have it we must. Use it we will. *(sits)*

(Delegates whisper and murmur; Christopher Campbell addresses Charlotte Woodward.)

CHRISTOPHER CAMPBELL: See there, Miss Woodward! They don't have the courage of their own convictions! The Resolution will never pass!

JAMES MOTT: Is there any further discussion before we call the question?

FREDERICK DOUGLASS: *(raises hand)* Sir!

JAMES MOTT: The chair recognizes Mr. Douglass.

FREDERICK DOUGLASS: *(stands)* All that distinguishes man as an intelligent and accountable being is equally true of woman. And if the government which governs by the free consent of the governed is truly just, there can be no reason in the world for denying to woman the exercise of the elective franchise, or a hand in making and administering the laws of the land. Our doctrine is that "right is of no sex." I urge this convention to support all of Mrs. Stanton's Resolutions — and most emphatically — Resolution Number Nine!

(Douglass sits and delegates applaud vigorously and shout.)

DELEGATES: Huzzah! Huzzah for Douglass and Stanton!

JAMES MOTT: *(bangs gavel)* Let us now vote. Those in favor of all Eleven Resolutions to the Declaration of Rights and Sentiments raise your hand.

(Elizabeth Cady Stanton, Frederick Douglass, Mary Ann McClintock, Charlotte Woodward, Martha Wright and lastly with great deliberation — Lucretia Mott — raise their right hand.)

JAMES MOTT: Those opposed?

(Male Delegate #1, Male Delegate #2, Female Delegate #1, Female Delegate #2, Jane Hunt raise their right hand.)

JAMES MOTT: The motion passes. The Resolutions are adopted. *All* of them!

(Delegates applaud politely.)

JAMES MOTT: We will now adjourn till half past seven, at which time we will reconvene and hear remarks on the subject of reform by Mrs. Lucretia Mott. *(bangs gavel)*

(Delegates go to table and sign Declaration, then exit right behind Christopher Campbell and Charlotte Woodward.)

CHRISTOPHER CAMPBELL: Don't tell me you're going to sign that absurd Declaration?

CHARLOTTE WOODWARD: If I had no hands, I would sign it with my feet! If I had no feet, I would sign it with my teeth!

(Charlotte Woodward crosses to table to sign; Christopher Campbell hails Frederick Douglass as Douglass passes by.)

CHRISTOPHER CAMPBELL: Mr. Douglass, this convention passed many resolutions. What chance do you think that any of them — especially the resolution urging women to seek the right to vote — will have to come true?

FREDERICK DOUGLASS: We are few in numbers, moderate in resources and very little-known in the world. The most we have to connect us is a firm commitment that we are in the right — and a firm faith that the right must ultimately prevail. *(exits right)*

(Charlotte Woodward passes by Christopher Campbell.)

CHRISTOPHER CAMPBELL: It was a pleasure to meet you, Miss Woodward. I thank you for a most interesting day.

CHARLOTTE WOODWARD: Be sure to put in your article, Mr. Campbell, that future generations will mark this day — July 20, 1848 — and this occasion as among the most important in the history of our great country. As important, perhaps, as that other day of indepedence in July, 1776.

CHRISTOPHER CAMPBELL: Indeed, Miss Woodward, I do believe in just treatment for the fairer sex. And man has much to be ashamed of in that regard. But giving women the right to vote! Really, Miss Woodward — women will vote the day man flies in the sky! *(laughs, exits right)*

CHARLOTTE WOODWARD: I *will* vote someday! And man can fly to the moon if he wants! *And* stay there! *(exits right)*

(LIGHTS DOWN CENTER AND RIGHT, LIGHTS UP LEFT ON Charlotte Woodward Pierce and Bridget Farrelly on bench at down left.)

BRIDGET FARRELLY: Golly, Mrs. Pierce, to have been present at such an exciting moment! If it hadn't been for women like you, I might not have been able to become a newspaper reporter. Women of our modern day owe so much to women like you!

CHARLOTTE WOODWARD PIERCE: You cannot look back, my dear. You have to keep looking forward. As Elizabeth Cady Stanton said:

(SPOTLIGHT ON Elizabeth Cady Stanton at down left.)

ELIZABETH CADY STANTON: We cannot bring about a moral revolution in a day or a year. But when men and women take time to think about a new question, the first step is taken.

(LIGHTS OUT)

THE END

RECYCLING: TAMING THE PLASTIC MONSTER!
(Physical Science)

Basic Concept:

This play introduces *recycling* — specifically the theory and process of recycling plastic — and explores related topics of pollution, landfills, toxins and the impact of recycling on the environment.

Pre- or Post-Play Activities:

- Have students go on a scavenger hunt around the school to find an example of each plastic type.

- Have students make posters detailing the seven categories of recycled plastic.

- Have students think of which common plastic materials might be used as bird houses and bird feeders — then make some!

- Have a contest for the most original art objects made from recycled plastic items.

- Take a trip to your local landfill where plastic garbage is buried and have the staff explain the landfill process.

Discussion Questions:

- How exactly do toxins from a landfill get into soil and water? Trace the pollution process from a single buried plastic bottle of bleach to your water faucet.

- Invite a local recycling or waste management representative to come to your class and talk about their work; how much money does your local government allocate to recycling and sanitation services?

- How is plastic made? Research the chemical process that converts petroleum, gas and coal into plastic.

STAGE SET: a school lunch room with a plastic table and 2 plastic chairs

CAST: 8 actors, min. 1 boy (•), 1 girl (+)

- + Saundra
- • Riley
  Students 1-6

EFFECT: sound — bell or buzzer ringing

PROPS: book; sunglasses; juice bottle; potato chips; potato chip container; plastic food dish; soft-drink bottle; laundry detergent bottle; vegetable oil bottle; bread bag; yogurt cup; styrofoam food container; large plastic bag containing these items — drinking straw; toothbrush; pill bottle; lid; egg carton; garden hose section; fishing line; sewing thread spool; packing peanuts

COSTUMES: characters wear contemporary school clothes with Saundra wearing a light jacket over her recycling code t-shirt; each Student 1–6 wears a t-shirt that has on the front a corresponding number inside the triangular plastic recycling code symbol — Student 1 has #1, Student #2 has 2, etc.; Saundra has #7 under her jacket

(LIGHTS UP FULL ON SAUNDRA and RILEY sitting at a lunch table at down center. Saundra is reading a book; Riley is eating lunch.)

SAUNDRA: Hi, Riley. I bet you a potato chip I can name more plastic things in this room than you can.

RILEY: You don't have a potato chip, Saundra.

SAUNDRA: I know — but you do, and I want one.

RILEY: *(offers a chip)* Well, here—

SAUNDRA: No! I want to earn it, not just have you give it to me!

RILEY: You sound like my parents. You're scaring me!

SAUNDRA: Come on, look around! Name whatever things you see made of plastic!

RILEY: Ummm, your sunglasses — the lenses and the frame.

SAUNDRA: This pen.

RILEY: This table.

SAUNDRA: These chairs.

RILEY: This juice bottle.

SAUNDRA: That potato chip container.

RILEY: Ummm, I can't think of any more.

SAUNDRA: No more? *(points)* How about that CD in Marsha's Walkman? *(points)* And the plastic knife and fork Derek is using to attack his spaghetti? *(points)* And the sack Deirdre's carrying her lunch in? *(points)* And the comb Benny's using to mess up his hair? And the gloves the food servers are wearing? And the covering over the ceiling lights? And Mr. Morton's hearing aid? And the trim on Darren's new sneakers? And Barbara's belt? And Monika's earrings? And Janna's tennis racket? And the fill inside your jacket? All of it plastic!

RILEY: Okay, okay, you win. Here's your chip! You earned it!

SAUNDRA: Thank you. *(regards chip thoughtfully)* What are you going to do with that plastic juice bottle when you're done with it?

RILEY: Toss it! I mean, in an approved waste container. I wouldn't *ever* litter.

SAUNDRA: Of course not. But do you know what happens to that bottle after you've put it in the trash?

RILEY: No, but I bet you're going to tell me.

(STUDENTS 1-3 enter from right and stand at down right; STUDENTS 4-6 enter from left and stand at down left; each Student carries a plastic object — Student 1, soft-drink bottle; Student 2, laundry detergent bottle; Student 3, vegetable oil bottle; Student 4, bread bag; Student 5, yogurt cup; Student 6, styrofoam food container.)

STUDENT 1: Recycling is the process of collecting, sorting and then re-making a waste item to be used again.

STUDENT 2: Either as a new product—

STUDENT 3: Or back to its original form.

STUDENT 4: Recycling helps preserve our environment and save natural resources.

RILEY: How?

STUDENT 5: By using less land for dumping our garbage. Each year in the United States, nearly three million acres of farmland and more than one hundred seventy thousand acres of wetland disappear.

STUDENT 6: Each day more than seven thousand acres of open space are lost forever.

SAUNDRA: Less waste means less pollution. And less pollution means a better world.

RILEY: Well, what is plastic, anyway? Why doesn't it just go away when you throw it in the trash?

STUDENT 1: The English word "plastic" comes from an ancient Greek word that means "to mold or to form."

STUDENT 2: Modern plastic is a material that is very easy to mold or form into any shape, size and color.

STUDENT 3: Plastic is made from a chemical compound called a *polymer* that is produced from oil.

STUDENT 4: Plastic is light in weight but very strong and durable.

STUDENT 5: And that's the problem with plastic — it just doesn't go away!

STUDENT 6: Americans use two-point-five million plastic bottles every hour!

STUDENT 1: Each person in the United States uses almost two hundred pounds of plastic a year!

STUDENT 2: Most of our plastic trash gets buried in land-fills.

STUDENT 3: Some plastic is *degradable*, meaning it will decay after a few months or years.

STUDENT 4: But most plastic never decays; when it's buried underground in a landfill, it can last forever!

STUDENT 5: And if the plastic contains *toxins* — or poi-sons — it can escape into the land and water and kill our crops and animals.

STUDENT 6: Recycling isn't just a good idea; it's a matter of life or death to the environment!

SAUNDRA: The plastics industry has worked hard to solve this problem. They developed a system that tells what kind of plastic something is made of. And that makes it easier to recycle!

RILEY: I see. Each type of plastic has its own number — like a code!

SAUNDRA: And you find the numbers stamped on the bottom of the bottle or printed on the package.

(Students 1-6 display their plastic item and the place where the code number is found.)

STUDENT 1: Code Number 1 is labeled PET. That's plastic made from a material called polyethylene terephthalate. It's used to make soft-drink and juice and water bottles.

STUDENT 2: Code Number 2 is labeled HDPE. That's plastic made from high-density polyethylene. It's used to make milk jugs and laundry detergent bottles.

STUDENT 3: Code Number 3 is labeled V. That's plastic made from vinyl and polyvinyl chloride. It's used to make vegetable oil bottles.

STUDENT 4: Code Number 4 is labeled LDPE. That's plastic made from low-density polyethylene. It's used to make dry cleaning bags and bread bags.

STUDENT 5: Code Number 5 is labeled PP. That's plastic made from polypropylene. It's used to make yogurt cups.

STUDENT 6: Code Number 6 is labeled PS. That's plastic made from polystyrene. It's used to make styrofoam food containers.

SAUNDRA: *(opens her jacket and displays t-shirt with #7)* And Code Number 7 is labeled "Other." That covers all the plastic made from all other materials. *(holds up a plastic food dish)* This microwave food dish, for example.

RILEY: That's all pretty cool. But what happens when this plastic juice bottle gets picked up from the recycling bin?

(Students 1–6 mime motions as they describe recycling process.)

STUDENT 1: When it gets to a recycling plant and has been sorted with other plastic items in its category, the bottle gets chopped up by a high-speed grinding machine.

STUDENT 2: Chopped up into little flakes and then cleaned off with a water spray machine.

STUDENT 3: The flakes are put into a giant tumble dryer and dried out.

STUDENT 4: These dried flakes may be melted down—

STUDENT 5: Or molded into long sticky strands—

STUDENT 6: Or shaped into tiny pellets.

SAUNDRA: The recycled plastic is made into new products.

RILEY: Such as?

STUDENT 1: Skis and surfboards.

STUDENT 2: Flower pots and automobile parts.

STUDENT 3: Pens and rulers.

STUDENT 4: Park bences and picnic tables.

STUDENT 5: Pipes and crates.

STUDENT 6: Filling for sleeping bags and carpet.

STUDENT 1: Pillows and jackets.

STUDENT 2: Yard fencing and house insulation.

STUDENT 3: Videotape cases.

STUDENT 4: Shopping bags.

STUDENT 5: Medicine capsules.

STUDENT 6: Food trays.

RILEY: And other new bottles.

SAUNDRA: Now you get the idea!

RILEY: Gosh, with recycling, we'd have all the plastic we needed. We'd never have to make any new plastic at all!

SAUNDRA: Unfortunately, only about one percent of all the plastic we use is recycled.

RILEY: That's crazy!

STUDENTS 1–6: But it's true!

RILEY: Well, what can we do to help people learn about recycling plastic?

SAUNDRA: You can find out how to recycle in your own community. Call your town or city government and ask about their recycling program.

STUDENT 1: And get your family and friends to recycle with you.

STUDENT 2: When you buy a plastic item, make sure it's marked with a recycling code number.

STUDENT 3: And try to buy things you're not going to just throw away after using once.

(Saundra draws a large plastic bag from behind table and pulls items from it, laying them on the table as they are announced by Students 1–6.)

SAUNDRA: Best of all — because it's the most fun — you can be your own plastic recycler, right in your own home!

STUDENT 4: Clean off your plastic drinking straws and use them to make mobiles and flower stems.

STUDENT 5: Use your recycled toothbrush as a stencil brush.

STUDENT 6: Use plastic lids as coasters.

STUDENT 1: Use egg cartons as extra ice cube trays or in the garden as seed starters for new plants.

STUDENT 2: Cut up your old garden hose and use it as a pail handle.

STUDENT 3: Or grips for your bicycle handlebars.

STUDENT 4: Fishing line is great for hanging things from your ceiling.

STUDENT 5: Sewing thread spools make great chess pieces.

STUDENT 6: And those packing peanuts? They make great stuffing for toys.

SAUNDRA: And don't forget about plastic milk bottles — they make great bird feeders!

(SOUND: Bell or buzzer rings. Students 1-3 begin exiting right, Students 4-6 begin exiting left.)

STUDENT 1: Oh, no, recess is over!

STUDENT 4: See you after school!

RILEY: Say, when we go back to class, why don't we see if our teacher will let us come up with ideas about how to make things out of recycled plastic?

SAUNDRA: That's a good idea. Because if we don't learn how to recycle, when we grow up, we'll be buried by our garbage!

RILEY: Lunch with you, Saundra, is always a learning experience.

(Saundra and Riley begin exiting left.)

SAUNDRA: Did you know that Americans create 190 million tons of garbage a year! That weighs more than thirty million elephants! Each one of us produces an average of almost four pounds of garbage a day!

(They exit; LIGHTS OUT.)

THE END

L.E. McCULLOUGH, PH.D. is an educator, playwright, composer and ethnomusicologist whose studies in music and folklore have spanned cultures throughout the world. Dr. McCullough is the Administrative Director of the Humanities Theatre Group at Indiana University-Purdue University at Indianapolis. Winner of the 1995 Emerging Playwright Award for his stage play *Blues for Miss Buttercup*, he is the author of *The Complete Irish Tinwhistle Tutor*, *Favorite Irish Session Tunes* and *St. Patrick Was a Cajun*, three highly acclaimed music instruction books, and has performed on the soundtracks for the PBS specials *The West*, *Lewis and Clark* and *Not for Ourselves Alone: The Story of Elizabeth Cady Stanton and Susan B. Anthony*. Since 1991 Dr. McCullough has received 43 awards in 31 national literary competitions and had 178 poem and short story publications in 90 North American literary journals. He is a member of The Dramatists Guild, American Conference for Irish Studies, Southeastern Theatre Conference and National Middle School Association. His books for Smith and Kraus include: *Plays of the Songs of Christmas*; *Stories of the Songs of Christmas*; *Ice Babies in Oz: Original Character Monologues*; *Plays of America from American Folklore, Vol. 1 & 2*; *Plays of the Wild West, Vol. 1 & 2*; *Plays from Fairy Tales*; *Plays from Mythology*; *Plays of People at Work*; *Plays of Exploration and Discovery*; *Anyone Can Produce Plays with Kids*; *Plays of Ancient Israel*; *Plays of Israel Reborn*; *111 One-Minute Monologues for Teens, Vol. 2* and *"Now I Get It!": 12 Ten-Minute Classroom Drama Skits for Elementary Science, Math, Language & Social Studies, Vol. 1 & 2*.